Praise for *Evangelist Marketing*

"I loved this book. I've often wondered why are there so few legendary marketing leaders? Alex Goldfayn tells the inside stories of the most brilliant campaigns, demystifies the magic, and reveals the first principles from these marketing giants."

—John Sculley, former Apple CEO

"Alex cuts into the muscle of consumer electronics companies and identifies what distinguishes the beloved brands from the me-too brands. He challenges the assembly line orientation of organizations and details how to win avidity with consumers. This is a look-yourself-in-mirror book for anyone that wants to escape the sea of sameness."

—Bob Stohrer, VP Marketing of Virgin Mobile

"In *Evangelist Marketing*, Alex Goldfayn reminds us that technology is merely a means to an end and that while great products and great experiences are the ultimate drivers of demand, it shouldn't stop there. To truly reach mass market status and not leave money on the table, companies must energize their marketing efforts to create 'evangelists' for their product or service. Alex' framework for reaching evangelist marketing nirvana is laid out in a clear step-by-step framework that if applied, will yield results."

—Chris Dobrec, Senior Director of Product Marketing, Cisco

"Alex Goldfayn doesn't pull any punches with *Evangelist Marketing*. Every high-tech marketer should read this book."

—Tony Lee, Vice President of Marketing, TiVo Inc.

"Alex nails right on the head one of the big issues in tech companies today: The fact that too often engineers run marketing. This creates complicated products that people don't really want and therefore don't buy. I think everyone in the tech industry should read this book, highlight key points and share them in their next product development meeting."

—Brian S. Packer, Managing Director of ZAGG International, the creators of Invisible Shield

"If you work with consumers, you should read this book. Alex demystifies the 'magic' that companies like Apple, Netflix, and Amazon tap into."

—Jon Dale, co-founder of Moolala

"Alex does a masterful job of pulling together insights across different products and businesses and then communicating those insights in a practical and useful way so you can see how they apply to your own situation and the issues you are facing."

—Eric Stang, CEO of Ooma

evangelist marketing

What Apple, Amazon, and Netflix Understand About Their Customers *(That Your Company Probably Doesn't)*

ALEX L. GOLDFAYN

BENBELLA

BenBella Books, Inc.
Dallas, Texas

BenBella

BenBella Books, Inc.
10300 N. Central Expressway
Suite #400
Dallas, TX 75231
benbellabooks.com
Send feedback to feedback@benbellabooks.com

Printed in the United States of America
10 9 8 7 6 5 4 3 2 1

Library of Congress Cataloging-in-Publication Data is available for this title.
ISBN 9781936661091

Editing by Erin Kelley
Copyediting by Debra Kirkby
Proofreading by Stacia Seaman and Michael Fedison
Cover design by Faceout Studio
Text design and composition by Silver Feather Design
Printed by Bang Printing

Distributed by Perseus Distribution
perseusdistribution.com
To place orders through Perseus Distribution:

Tel: 800-343-4499
Fax: 800-351-5073
E-mail: orderentry@perseusbooks.com

Dedication

To my dad, who taught me the magical combination of hard work and perseverance.

And to my mom, who is my biggest evangelist.

Acknowledgments

This book would not exist without the hard work and support of my agent, Joelle Delbourgo. She has sat on every possible side of the publisher's desk (can a desk have six sides?), and I am grateful for her experience, advice, and belief.

Thanks to Glenn Yeffeth, who runs BenBella Books. I'm sure glad that he got into publishing after a successful career in the consulting world. There's no one better suited to lead this book into the world than Glenn. His team, which includes the talented Jennifer Canzoneri, Erin Kelley, and Debra Kirkby, is also first class. Thanks to you all for your hard work and support.

My thanks also to all of my clients—I learn what I teach from you. And I very much appreciate the contributions of the ten industry leaders and thinkers who contributed their experiences and perspectives while I was writing this book: Geoffrey Moore, Bob Stohrer, Steve Swasey, Jef Holove, John Sculley, Tony Lee, Guy Kawasaki, Brian Packer, Chris Dobrec, and Glenn Rogers.

A critical life lesson for me is that anything worth achieving requires perseverance; some activities (like, say, writing a book) demand high doses of ambition and perseverance. I learned both of these traits from my parents, Leon and Jane Goldfayn, who have taught me a lot in my life, but this lesson of creative persistence may be the most valuable of all. Thanks to the rest of my family for your endless support: Jan, Ron, Keith, and especially the family matriarch, the lovely and beautiful Bella.

Finally, I must express my enormous gratitude to my wife and life partner, Lisa. I thank my lucky stars every day for her grace, elegance, and unconditional support. In dealing with me and raising our two amazing children, Noah and Bella, she works much harder than I do. Thank you for every little thing that you do.

Contents

PART FOUR: THE COMMUNICATIONS

PART FIVE: CONSUMER EVANGELISM

Write to Me

If you have a question or a comment as you read this book, feel free to send it directly to me by email at alex@technologytailor.com. I will reply to every email personally.

Introduction

This book is for anyone in the business of consumer electronics: whether you work for a large manufacturer or are attempting to build a startup, whether you're a marketer or an engineer, whether you're a CEO or a customer service representative, whether you work for the manufacturer itself or one of its agencies. Reading this book and implementing the improvements I lay out will help you sell more consumer electronics products. But it will also do much more: if you execute only a few of the many fast, easy, and downright affordable steps I present here, you will create a loyal and passionate consumer following—evangelists rather than customers.

What Is a Consumer Evangelist?

The word *evangelist* is thought to have developed from a similar word in Koine Greek, a form of Greek spoken between 300 B.C. and A.D.300 Roughly translated, the Koine Greek root from which evangelist comes means *the bringing of good news*. The verb form means *to proclaim*.

Some of the first evangelists were biblical, like the writers of the Four Gospels in the New Testament: Matthew, Mark, Luke, and John. In the Bible, evangelism is described as "spreading the gospel"—believers educating, exciting, and convincing nonbelievers.

In more modern times, churches have long had evangelist members, who move from home to home, person to person, spreading the gospel and, well... evangelizing.

In the corporate world, there have long been two types of evangelists: the first type is the employed evangelists, who are the executives or managers whose job it is to "spread the company gospel" to the outside world. Recently, we have seen high-level positions created with the word evangelist in the title. Google has had at least one "chief evangelist" on staff since 2005. These people are easy to create, and by now, they are an expected part of corporate culture. These people are not the focus of our book, given that they get paid to evangelize.

The second type, customer evangelists, are the people who spend money on something, use it, like it, think about it, use it some more, begin to love it, and then begin to communicate their love. The more they communicate, the more they believe, and the more they love. A critical mass of mainstream evangelists can change the world forever for a company, but they are very difficult to acquire. They are the focus of this book.

In this book, I will educate you on how to develop evangelist customers in the consumer technology space. These evangelists have very specific traits.

- *They are mainstream consumers.* They are not early adopters, although plenty of early adopters are evangelists. For reasons I will describe later in this book, early adopters are not the kind of evangelist (or even customer) you want. Mainstream consumers are surrounded by a network of other mainstream consumers; those are the people you want backing (and buying) your product. They love your products—not like—love.
- *They are passionate.* Evangelists' enthusiasm for your product is off the charts. They think and talk about your products with a level of energy that rivals that of die-hard sports fans.
- *They are thrilled about how your product improves their lives.* They perceive very high value from your device, which exceeds their expectations. They cannot imagine life without your product, and wonder how they lived for so long without it.

- *They are news hunters.* They seek out information about your new product releases. They participate in communities with like-minded individuals. They discuss the ins and outs of your products with friends, family, colleagues, retail clerks, and strangers they encounter using your product (*Don't you just love your iPad?*).
- *They are communicators.* They talk to people about how wonderful your products are, and they are the foundation of your word-of-mouth buzz generation efforts.
- *They are your public defenders.* They will try to change others' negative outlooks or remedy their poor experiences with your devices. If someone is speaking negatively of your device or your company, your evangelists counter that with positive energy.
- *They are trusting.* If you say it is so, your evangelists tend to believe you. They believe you are looking out for their best interests.
- *They are forgiving.* Product errors? Embarrassing public relations? Security risks? No problem. Your evangelists perceive these issues as accidents, occurring unintentionally. The good always outweighs the drawbacks for evangelists.
- *They are hyper-repeat customers.* Some people read every book their favorite author writes. Evangelists buy as many of your products as possible. You are their favorite author. If you make it, they will buy it.

Now, look at this list, and tell me why you shouldn't be spending every ounce of energy developing customer evangelists.

I can teach you how, but it won't be easy. I argue that creating evangelists in consumer electronics is more difficult than in any other industry for many reasons, including mainstream customers' continuing lack of comfort with technology and the overwhelming number of choices for technology products in the marketplace. Companies are updating their products so quickly that it's extremely difficult to create an energized customer base around a product that will only be the latest model for six to twelve months.

Why I'm Writing This Book

People ask me: *Why are you writing this book? Why do you care? Don't you think tech companies are doing pretty well?*

Yes, I say, they're doing well enough. But they're also leaving billions of dollars on the table. Tens of billions. Because the marketing—which must be incredibly powerful to develop mainstream evangelists—is atrocious in our business. That's right. Huge companies—Hewlett-Packard, Dell, AT&T, Samsung, Panasonic, Microsoft, and nearly every other company in our business (at least 98 percent of all consumer electronics manufacturers)—run by millionaire executives with graduate degrees from the most respected universities in the land are succeeding *in spite* of their marketing, not *because* of it. Consumers have an intense natural interest in technology—more so than in any other industry besides sports. But not only are these companies not capitalizing on it, the harmful marketing actually drives away customers who'd likely buy their products if they said nothing at all.

How do I know all this?

I was a syndicated technology columnist at the *Chicago Tribune* for five years and hosted a tech radio show on Midwest powerhouse WGN-AM for four years. I've been on the receiving end of thousands of press releases, have interviewed technology executives in the thousands, and have talked to thousands of consumers about their use and perceptions of technology. Since my media years, I've worked with many of the largest technology manufacturers in the world as a private consultant and adviser, speaker, and spokesperson.

For years, I've had deep insight into what technology makers are doing to market their products, and how consumers perceive that marketing. I've seen the rather massive disconnect between consumers and the executives trying to sell technology to them. They think about the same technology very differently. They use different language. Consumers have told me what they'd like to see from manufacturers in terms of marketing, communication, and education—and I've watched company after company invest millions of dollars not delivering it.

So yes, the industry is doing well enough. But only a few companies have passion in the mainstream. Every other manufacturer simply has fleeting users. That means a select few firms—just three—are creating extraordinary marketing, while everyone else's marketing is ordinary at best and suicidal at worst.

If you're reading this and you're connected to a consumer electronics company, that company is likely leaving millions or billions of dollars on the table.

This book will teach you how to move that money off the table and into your bank account.

As I see it, only five products—made by just three companies—have a critical mass of mainstream consumer evangelists:

- The iPhone® mobile digital device
- The iPad® mobile digital device
- The Mac® computer
- The Amazon Kindle® electronic book
- Netflix® video streaming service

Always remember that success in consumer electronics comes to those companies that develop a critical mass of *mainstream* consumer evangelists. I am sure that many companies have some highly technical early-adopter evangelists, but their networks mostly consist of other tech types. Parents with jobs and responsibilities are generally not getting their tech recommendations from early adopters who religiously read tech blogs and message boards. In this book, my focus is strictly on the mainstream—which is where your focus needs to be as well.

I will never argue with you if you say, *But there are lots of other companies that have evangelists, Alex*. I would say you are absolutely right. Google has evangelists but not as many, and not as energized as Apple's, Amazon's, and Netflix's customers. Facebook has evangelists, but would they remain evangelical if there was a cost to use the site? I have my doubts. Twitter has evangelists, but they are not really mainstream consumers. Zappos, the Internet shoe retailer, has evangelists, but it's not a critical mass of mainstream customers. The people who use Zappos love it. But there are not nearly as many moms, dads, grandmas, and grandpas who use Zappos as those who buy Apple's products or Amazon's Kindle content or pay for a Netflix subscription every month.

So here's the point: many companies in the consumer electronics space have *some* evangelists. That's great. It's a terrific start. This is not an all-or-nothing process. Companies cannot go directly from Point A—having no customer evangelists—to Point B—having a critical mass of mainstream evangelists. This is a continuum, with many steps in between Point A and Point B. It's a process.

I believe that only Apple, Amazon, and Netflix have reached the ultimate conclusion in the process, but even they must repeatedly do the right things to maintain this position. For example, we witnessed the emotional reaction—and the resulting financial ramifications—when Netflix increased prices on its DVD and streaming subscription plans in 2011. Gravity pushes backwards in consumer electronics. Do nothing, or the wrong things, and you'll quickly lose ground.

This book is your road map for the journey between where you are now and that critical mass of mainstream consumer evangelists.

Bon voyage and good luck!

A Note on Improvement

This book presents a rather encompassing system for technology companies to develop mainstream consumer evangelists. However, as you likely know, improvement is not all or nothing. It's incremental. So, my advice is to select a couple of techniques from this book, focus on them, and move them forward. You'll be moving your products, brand, and company toward a critical mass of mainstream consumers. Once you've implemented these areas into your work or company, then start integrating the next improvement or two.

Further, don't forget to maintain the things you're doing right while developing the new skills you learn in this book. If you don't maintain your strengths, they'll atrophy. Competition will pass you by.

You don't suddenly wake up with a critical mass of mainstream customer evangelists. You have to do the right things successfully and consistently to develop them. So, the goal is to move in the right direction daily. Take small steps consistently through this system, and you'll get to where you want to go.

Insights from Industry Insiders

• • • • •

Given that an integral part of my philosophy is that you need to talk to your customers constantly (in the form of qualitative interviews) to gather insights and deeply understand how they think about technology and your products, I've had lengthy conversations with ten consumer electronics executives and leaders during the course of writing this book. Some of them are my clients, and all of them are people I admire. I carefully selected this group of ten because of their inventive thinking. Throughout this book, you'll find their thoughts on various aspects of the problems in consumer electronics and my process for creating consumer evangelists, along with my analysis of their positions, in boxes like this one.

A Note on Change

Consumer electronics moves at lightning speed, and since I started writing this book over a year ago, (which is about 17 years in tech time), a lot has changed has changed in the industry:

- Steve Jobs passed away.
- Cisco did away with one of the most popular consumer electronics products on the planet, the Flip video camera.
- Netflix raised prices, rolled out a new brand called Qwikster for its DVD business, and then killed it before it ever saw the light of day.

I want to focus on the third item, since Netflix is featured on the cover of this book for what it does right. The company's vice president of corporate communications, Steve Swasey, is featured prominently in this book. I think Steve, his CEO, Reed Hastings, and the VP of Marketing at Netflix, Leslie Kilgore, are as good a consumer technology leadership team as exists in the business. Remember, these executives are dealing with managing a company transitioning from a lovable startup to the Microsoft of its category almost overnight.

But the company did not have a good year in 2011.

First, it raised prices on many customers by about 60 percent. The cost of renting one DVD at a time and unlimited streaming went from $10 per month to $16. Then, in the fall, Netflix spun off its DVD business, renaming it Qwikster, a Netflix company.

Consumer reacted predictably: more than 1 million fled the company's DVD and streaming arm according to the most recent earnings call Netflix held at the time of this late writing.

Soon after, Netflix abandoned its plans to split its business in two, and brought everything back under the Netflix umbrella.

Here are the lessons, as I see them, from the company's recent missteps. Ironically, this list turns out to be a preview of some of the advice and warnings I lay out in-depth later in this book.

- Success is fleeting in consumer electronics. In fact, gravity pushes backwards. Just because you've attained a critical mass of customers—evangelists in Netflix's case—doesn't mean they're with you no matter what. This is not a marriage. Consumers are constantly evaluating their choices. *You have to continue giving people new reasons to stay with you.*
- You must keep doing the right things, constantly. This means that you should be innovating not only your products and services, but also your marketing. Powerful new messages communicated from the right platforms are key.
- The results of your marketing should never surprise you. Netflix admitted that more people left the service than the company expected. That's because Netflix, which prides itself on customer insights, didn't ask enough of its members about what they'd do if the price went up by 60 percent. If they asked say, 1,000 people, they would have learned that many would have been angry enough to abandon ship.

If you're in the marketing business, the single most important and powerful action you can take is talking to your customers. Taking action based on the thoughts and feelings of your customers guarantees success in our business. Without customer input, you're just guessing from a conference room.

Much more on all of this in the coming pages.

Sitting here in the fall of 2011, I think there's plenty of time for Netflix to right its ship. I also think that to do so, the company must take real steps to placate angry customers. This probably means extending a special offer to its current customers—at this point, some people need a reason to stay. Further, Netflix must get back to doing the things that took it to the top of the consumer electronics mountain: talk to customers and take action based on their insights.

Alex Goldfayn

October, 2011

Resources

I've created a variety of resources to supplement the material in this book. Many of these tools are at your disposal at no cost. You can go to my Web site (http://www.technologytailor.com) and click on the image of the book cover to see the complete, current list of tools. As I complete the writing of this book, I've assembled a number of resources.

Go to http://www.facebook.com/EvangelistMarketing to interact with me and others—including your peers and colleagues—about effective marketing of consumer electronics. I'll also provide exclusive content specifically for this page on a regular basis. This is also where I'll periodically offer assessments, evaluations, and consulting, done personally by me, for your brand and products, at no cost. It's my way of thanking you for reading this book.

Go to my Web site to sign up for my *Evangelist Marketing Minute*, a free, weekly, thinking launch point that will take you no more than one minute to read and think about. It's delivered by email every Monday.

I've also created an *Evangelist Marketing* video series, with lessons that focus on successful consumer electronics marketing. Access it by visiting my Web site and clicking on the image of this book.

My blog, *Creating Consumer Evangelists* (http://www.consumerevangelists.com), features my latest thinking on this topic, and is updated several times each week.

part one

The Epidemic and the Miracle Cure

one

Good News and Bad News: You're Leaving Billions on the Table

If you work in consumer electronics, you're very lucky, because there is no other industry in business with such a captive, passionate, and interested audience. That's the good news.

The bad news is that you're not capitalizing fully on this interest. In fact, the success the industry enjoys (and by success, I mean sales) has nearly everything to do with the intense public interest in your products and very little to do with your marketing, advertising, or public relations outreach. If it weren't for this built-in consumer and media interest, the entire industry—from computing to smartphones to televisions to popular Web sites—would only be generating a fraction of its current sales.

That's because, almost universally, consumer electronics marketing, advertising, and public relations are all terrible. They're boring. They're far too technical. They don't capture consumers' imaginations, and usually not even their attention. Every single company in consumer electronics is missing opportunities.

At best, you're leaving money on the table. At worst, your marketing or public relations departments are single-handedly ruining your multibillion-dollar research and development investments.

In consumer electronics, most products to hit the mainstream market are excellent. But most of the marketing meant to promote these products actually damages their chances at retail.

This book will identify the areas in which your marketing is falling short—your language, your process, and your people, to name just three areas—and then arm you with a proven system focused on knowing your consumer deeply, perfecting the language that you use, and identifying the platforms from which you communicate. Execute the steps laid out here, and you'll create passionate, intensely loyal mainstream consumers—your evangelists.

For now, let's get back to the good news.

Technology Is Like Sports

Technology consumers are like sports fans: they're highly interested, passionate, and devoted to following developments—sometimes daily—from a slew of news sources. They range from industry observers who regularly read articles (fair-weather fans) to enthusiastic supporters (die-hards) of their adopted "home team" tech makers. The best marketers in consumer electronics are home teams, and some of their die-hard fans are the evangelists you'll read so much about in this book. People treat their favorite manufacturers as though these companies' devices are representing them—just like their favorite sports team. Apple has die-hard fans. Blackberry has die-hard fans. Amazon does, too. Comcast does not. Dell doesn't (but it used to).

Sports has talk radio. Consumer electronics has review sites, like Amazon and CNet, where consumers share praise and anger about their favorite devices. Sports has box scores. Technology has Sunday ads and e-commerce sites, where each week's prices are tracked as if they were a game line.

But the comparison only begins with consumers. Like sports, the technology market enjoys intense media coverage. Daily newspapers have dedicated technology reporters. Many have columnists (I was one for nearly five years at the *Chicago Tribune*). Many radio stations have technology radio shows (I hosted one on one of the largest stations in America, WGN). Most morning news programs regularly do tabletop technology segments. There are terrific tech news Web sites like CNet, and incredibly detailed blogs like *Gizmodo* and *Engadget*, which follow the tech news and product releases of the day by the minute.

There's another element responsible for the intense consumer interest that's unique to technology: the fear of being left behind one's peers, which doesn't happen in any other industry. Automobiles come close, but new cars come annually, predictably, and comfortably. Everybody knows that if they purchase a new car in March, by next February a new model will be out, but the car that was previously purchased isn't outdated. New technology is released far more frequently. Buy a TV or laptop today, and it may well be outdated in a month or two—maybe even next week. Yesterday I paid for the newest, but tomorrow there may be something newer. This is uncomfortable, so consumers do their best to keep up with the latest technology.

It's a perfect storm of interest, really: passionate customers and highly involved media charged with feeding consumer interest. You couldn't ask for anything more. For this, as an industry, we're incredibly lucky. What other consumer industry enjoys such built-in, captive interest? There isn't one. When a tech company releases a new product, it's easy to alert consumers because there is a huge range of available media to leverage.

FIGURE 1.1
How Technology Is Like Sports

IN SPORTS	IN CONSUMER ELECTRONICS
Die-hard fans	Passionate supporters of one manufacturer over another (example: Using a Blackberry over an iPhone)
Fantasy football/baseball participants	Intensely interested consumers who read everything they can get their hands on: mostly online, many times on message boards
Reading the box score	Browsing the Sunday big-box ads
Catching the game	Going to local retailer to touch and feel technology
Talk radio	Consumer reviews on sites like Amazon (and talk radio!)
Beat writers and columnists in daily publications	Tech reporters and columnists in daily publications
Dedicated Web sites for favorite teams	Dedicated Web sites for favorite gadgets or brands

Your "Marketing" Is Undermining You

This leads me once more to the bad news: the problem is that, despite this incredibly rare opportunity to feed intense consumer interest through seemingly endless platforms, as an industry, we are doing a terrible job at it.

In fact, the marketing and public relations efforts that many consumer electronics makers currently undertake actually undermine their success. Let's put it another way: if technology companies did away with their consumer marketing and communications programs, they'd likely see little difference in their sales because the technology media would still be covering the industry and consumers would still be clamoring for information.

Ironically, I believe it's precisely because the consumer electronics industry has so much interest from consumers that companies have become complacent about their marketing and communications. Here are eleven of the most common mistakes that marketing and communications departments make that undermine your company's success. These are the mistakes that are costing you billions.

Most mainstream technology manufacturers:

- Don't understand what customers want from their category of product.
- Don't know how consumers think about their products.
- Never learn the words their customers use when describing their products.
- Dismiss consumers from their marketing strategy formulation other than through some quantitative research and impersonal focus groups.
- Use bland, sometimes scary, highly technical language.
- Inadvertently allow their engineers to shape their communication
- Assign product names that act as a roadblock to creating passionate consumer fans.
- Create horrific press releases.

- Miss out on countless opportunities with the media.
- Put their most inexperienced employees (media communications associates) in charge of external communications.
- Focus far too much on social media.

Industry Marketing vs. Evangelist Marketing: Sony

➤ ➤ ➤

This section will appear periodically throughout the book. It will show how various companies in the consumer electronics industry are approaching the marketing of their products—including device names, descriptions, and language—along with my suggestions for streamlining and perfecting this approach to facilitate the development of mainstream consumer evangelists.

Industry Marketing

Here are the first two paragraphs of Sony's product description of its video game console on Amazon:

> The fourth generation of hardware released for the PlayStation 3 entertainment platform, the PlayStation 3 160GB system is the next stage in the evolution of Sony's console gaming powerhouse. Loaded with a mix of multimedia features and functions available on earlier PlayStation 3 models, as well as a series of new advancements and refinements, the PlayStation 3 160GB system is destined to push the envelope in the realm of Next-Generation entertainment.

What's Under the Hood

As with previous models, the PlayStation 3 160GB system features an IBM "Cell" processor and a co-developed NVIDIA graphics processor that together allow the system to perform two trillion calculations per second. Yet the 160GB system manages to improve on this with its 45nm version of the processor, which although running at the same 60+nm speed as previous PS3 versions, uses less energy. This makes the unit's smaller size and quieter fan possible. Along with the traditional AV and composite connections, the 160GB system also boasts an HDMI (High-Definition Multimedia Interface) port, which delivers uncompressed, unconverted digital picture and sound to 149 compatible high-definition TVs and projectors. (The system is capable of 128-bit pixel precision and 1080p resolution for a full HD experience) This console also provides for an extreme sound experience by supporting Dolby Digital 5.1, DTS 5.1, as well as Linear PCM 7.1. Finally, it features cross connectivity with your PC network and PlayStation Portable (PSP) and its pre-installed, 160GB hard disc drive allows you to save games as well as download content from the Internet. Unlike some other models of The PlayStation 3, the 160GB system does not offer backwards compatibility.

Evangelist Marketing

There's far too much emphasis on technical specifications here, and nearly nothing about how the PS3 will improve its prospective customers' lives. How in the world will mainstream customers, moms and dads, get through that lingo? Here's how I'd attack the first paragraph:

CONTINUED ON FOLLOWING PAGE . . .

CONTINUED . . .

The PlayStation 3 revolutionizes your time in the family room. You probably already know about our video games, which are best in class because our technology is so advanced. But did you know the PS3 is the only video game console that plays Blu-ray discs? And did you know we have Netflix built in, so you can stream thousands of movies over the Internet? Oh, and you can use a PS3 to browse the Web, listen to music, and everything happens in brilliant 1080p high definition and Dolby stereo sound.

My version focuses on the consumer, not the technology. Mine would sell more Playstations to mainstream consumers.

Consumers Are Missing from Your Consumer Marketing

These problems are so common because the process most companies use to develop their marketing (including language, messaging, communications, and consumer education) is fundamentally and consistently flawed. This is how marketing strategy development flows in most consumer electronics companies:

FIGURE 1.2

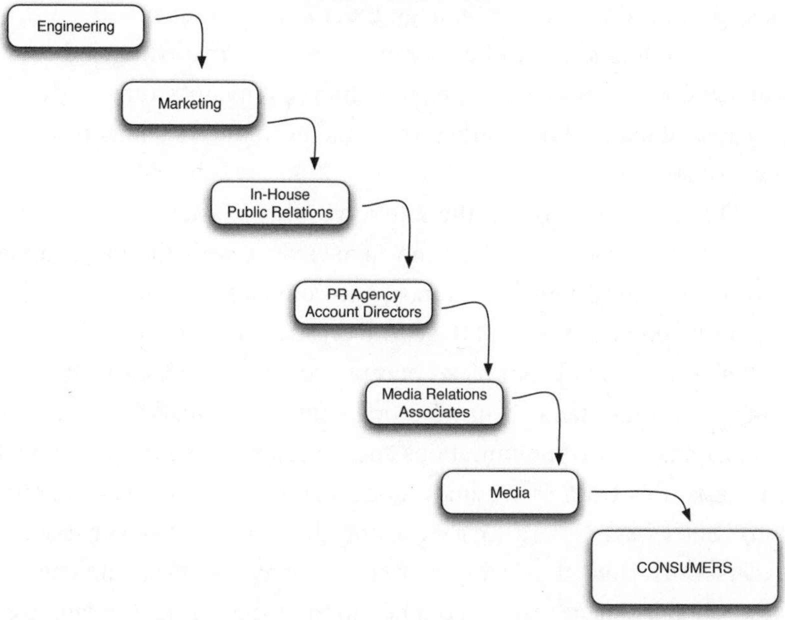

Marketing formulation always begins with the engineering department because this is where your products are created. These are the people who put together the technical pieces, and make them work, which is why they're the first people to introduce new devices within most companies. Not only that, but engineers usually name the new products. Engineers detail the products' features. They demonstrate them to the company executives and marketing leaders. Engineers discuss the products' technical aspects in terms that make perfect sense to them. The marketers ask lots of questions and eventually they begin to understand how the product works as well. The marketing department then takes this highly technical, all-but-impossible-to-understand information from engineering and molds it for their in-house public relations department, which tweaks it a bit and sends it to the contracted PR agency account directors, who pass it on to inexperienced media relations people, who blast terrible press releases to an overwhelmed, attention-deficit-disordered media. The media—online and offline—accepts a tiny percentage of these terribly written, offensively uninteresting press releases and, because they need to cover technology, cover it for consumers.

This is the sad story of consumer electronics marketing and communications for most mainstream technology manufacturers. This is the cause of many of the marketing problems in the consumer technology industry.

The rest of this book is the solution to this problem.

Note that consumers have no involvement with the formulation of your marketing, which is supposed to convince consumers. Instead, the most technical people in the entire organization—the ones who are least able to simplify complex concepts so that the mainstream consumer can understand them—are originating your marketing strategy and shaping your communications and language. Marketing executives may resist this truth (sometimes, understandably, out of self-preservation), but I have a hard time believing that well-educated marketing leaders can create the highly technical, overly complex, difficult-to-understand language that's so common in the industry. No, this language starts with the people who are comfortable with it—engineers. Everyone else between them and consumers is left to try to make sense of it.

"If I Build This You Will Definitely Want It"

"Most of the large consumer electronics companies have engineers running their marketing. They don't have a clue, and frankly they're a little arrogant. They don't know what the consumer wants. They're not listening to the people buying their product. They think, *if I build this you will definitely want it*, instead of paying attention to what the consumers actually want. It's against their grain to learn how to solicit customer feedback and get involved with their consumers and understand what consumers actually want.

Do these companies know they're bad marketers?

"They don't. They actually think that marketers are a lower life form. They don't understand there's a lot of science to it. They think marketing is putting out good-looking ads."

—Brian Packer, Managing Director, ZAGG International, maker of the InvisibleShield

Alex's Analysis: It makes perfect sense to me that engineers will not succeed at marketing. What makes absolutely no sense to me is how multibillion-dollar companies have allowed their engineers to shape, mold, directly influence, and in many cases, actually run the marketing and consumer outreach they do. Would you let people with marketing degrees engineer the guts of your products? Would you let your public relations team debug your software? Also, Brian makes a fascinating point about awareness: many in the industry don't consciously realize that this phenomenon is occurring. Or they do, and just don't see it as a problem. It is a big, ugly, expensive problem. And it has to stop.

Note also that communication flows one way—downhill, through many departments, exiting your firm's control, and entering the public domain via the work of people who are essentially press release blasters. Your media relations folks do little other than distributing thousands of press releases and taking requests for interviews. The most inexperienced people in your entire organization are distributing the language of the most technical people in your firm. I'll have much more on your media relations people in Chapter 9.

My system for creating consumer electronics evangelists, laid out step by step in this book, turns this process upside down. Here's what the ideal marketing and language development approach looks like in my process:

FIGURE 1.3

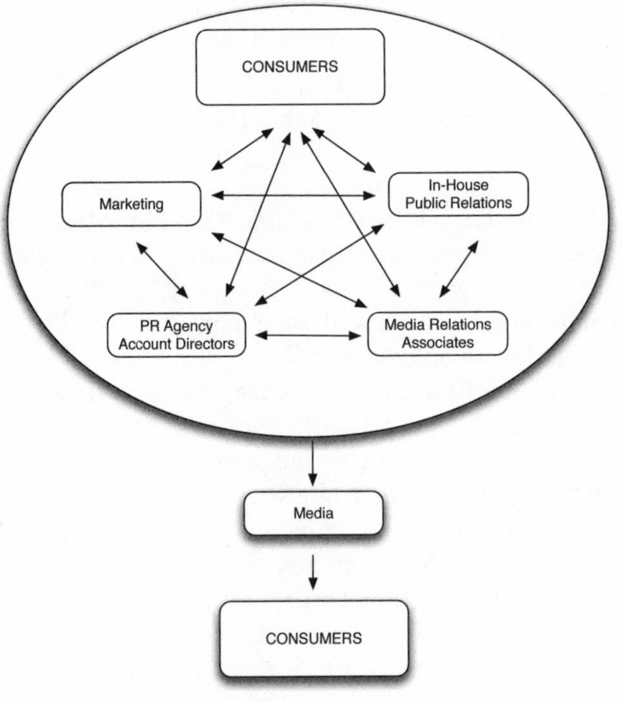

Instead of engineers, my system begins (and ends) with consumers. The best language to convince potential customers comes from current customers. How do you find out how your customers talk about your products? You ask them. And I'm not talking about focus groups. I'm suggesting deep, qualitative interviews with consumers. (I also advise my clients that people in every department of their organization should have a five-minute conversation with their customers every day. Imagine the insights. Imagine the opportunities your organization will create if each person spent just a fraction of the time that is wasted online each day with your customers instead.) Chapter 7 covers consumer-interviewing techniques in depth. If technology makers simply repeated the language of their customers—which would cost a lot less than the broken process most companies use today—the industry would be generating much more revenue.

All departments involved with distributing marketing and communication, including public relations—in-house and agencies—should be involved in the creation of your marketing. Your public relations department is often the launch point of your carefully crafted messages—when your messaging goes from conference rooms into the real world. As such, PR people are often the first to understand what messaging works and what doesn't. More than any other department in your company, your public relations team can predict what messaging will resonate and what will not. However, I've rarely seen PR involved in crafting strategy. Rather, at most technology companies, PR simply receives marching orders and is asked to execute them. Public relations professionals are the worker bees to the marketing people's queen bees. In this case, the workers can teach the queen a thing or two about what the real world is really like.

Instead of flowing downhill, one department at a time, marketing development should be an inclusive, 360-degree process. The insights will come from consumers without difficulty. But the molding of these insights into usable strategy must come from every department involved in external communications. So instead of the one-way flow that is accepted in so many organizations, my system creates a dynamic, multidisciplinary approach to strategy creation, in which the ultimate beneficiaries are consumers and, in turn, the manufacturer, which finds it easier than ever to sell electronics to an educated, motivated consumer public.

If you arrange your strategy creation in this way, you'll go to the marketplace with a powerful, cohesive message with language developed from the insights of your customers. What you say about your products—from ads to press releases, from your product packaging to your product manual—will be infinitely more effective than what you're saying now because this communication was not only developed by the right people, it originated from the right people: your consumers.

Chapter Summary

- Bad marketing is causing you to leave millions or billions of dollars on the table.
- Consumers and the media have a huge interest in consumer electronics. They follow technology developments like they follow their favorite sports team.
- Most consumer electronics companies start their marketing process with their engineers—exactly the wrong people for this.
- Consumers are missing from your marketing: they should be the centerpiece, but they are almost never involved in the creation of marketing strategy in our business.

two

Your Success Depends on a Series of Shifts

Psychologically, business success often comes from a series of mindset or perception shifts. Consumer technology is no different. This chapter covers the three major shifts required to improve your marketing, branding, and communications dramatically. This is a big-picture chapter. It focuses on perceptions: yours, your teams', and your customers'. We begin with perceptions because they guide everything we do—and, for that matter, everything your staff, partners, and customers do.

But first, let's look at one shift that you should not make: do not change your approach to developing your products. My experience in this business has been that if your product (or your client's product) has made it to the mainstream market, it's almost always good enough. Good enough for what? Good enough to provide value to consumers. Generally, most consumer electronics do what they say they do fairly well. I've rarely heard about consumers being truly angry about a mainstream product they've purchased because it doesn't do what you say. Sometimes people get upset because they get a defective device or they have trouble with customer service or a return. But functionality is usually not your problem. And this book is not about customer service or quality control.

However, it is about your marketing, branding, communication, and education efforts. And you will lay the groundwork for improving these areas dramatically if you succeed in the shifts in perception discussed in this chapter. Even a small shift, say, just 10 percent in the right direction, will be a big step toward success. This is an important point: these shifts are not all or nothing, black or white. Small improvements are valuable. A series of movements of 1 or 2 percent in the right direction will add up to significant improvement.

This chapter discusses the three shifts required for most high-tech companies to begin the process of developing passionate, loyal, energetic, and incredibly supportive customers:

1. Shifting your own mindset: The changes you have to make about how you perceive your company and your products.
2. Shifting your view of marketing strategy formulation: The changes your company (or employer or client) has to make.
3. Shifting your consumer perceptions: The resulting changes in your customers' perceptions. The goal of the first two shifts is to create this third shift.

We begin with the most important shift in mindset: your own.

Shifting Your Mindset

This is not only the most important shift but the most difficult one as well. I'm asking you to change how you think about what you do. I'm asking you to stop thinking about your company as a product manufacturer and begin thinking about yourself as a consumer lifestyle improver. Here are the three main components of shifting your own mindset:

FIGURE 2.1

Shifting Your Mindset

Along Three Continua

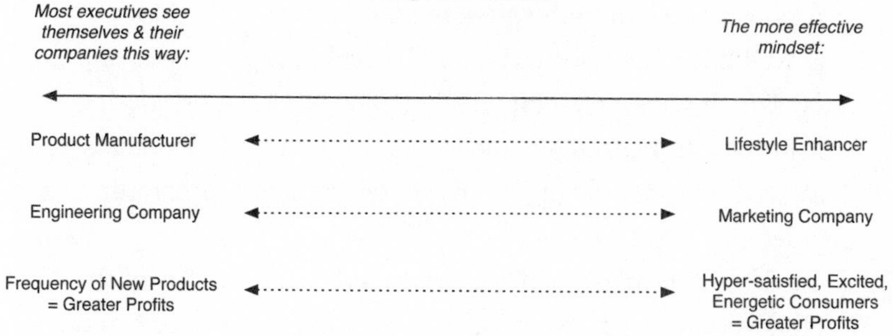

Shift Toward Lifestyle Enhancement

How you think of yourself and your company shapes everything you do in any business but especially in ours. Too many companies in consumer electronics think of themselves as product makers instead of customer lifestyle improvers. You can tell immediately how a company thinks of itself by looking at their outgoing communications—including their ads and press releases, as well as the interviews their executives give. For example, judging from its robot television commercials for the Droid in 2009 and 2010, Motorola clearly thinks of itself as a product manufacturer. (As an aside, I think those commercials were brutal, and that the Droid smartphones have been succeeding in spite of the commercials that advertise them—more on this later.) Further, Dell's print ads over the years have always clearly declared that the company sees itself as a product maker first. These ads prominently depict computers and peripherals, along with their technical specifications. For many years, these advertisements were on the backs of popular magazines, fold-out style.

Let's look at Motorola, which launched its XOOM™ tablet device in early 2011 to compete with Apple's iPad. The company's press release about the tablet's availability on the Verizon Wireless network states that the XOOM tablet "won the coveted CNET Best of Show award at the 2011 Consumer Electronics Show for being 'the most potentially disruptive technology.'" The rest of the release is all tech specifications, all the time:

> A powerhouse in both software and hardware, the Motorola XOOM is built around a 1GHz dual-core processor and 10.1-inch widescreen HD display. The sleek, stylish design features a front-facing 2-megapixel camera for video chats, as well as a rear-facing 5-megapixel camera that captures video in 720p HD.
>
> The Motorola XOOM showcases the innovations of the Honeycomb user experience that improves on Android favorites such as widgets, multitasking, browsing, notifications, and customization, as well as featuring the latest Google Mobile services. The Motorola XOOM also features full support for tabbed browsing and support for the Adobe Flash Player, available soon as a free download, to enjoy all the video and other rich content available on the Web. For additional information about upgrading their XOOM to 4G LTE, customers can visit www.verizon.com/Xoom4GLTE-Upgrade starting Thursday, Feb. 24.

You can see what's important to Motorola here: the gadgetry, the engineering. Motorola sees itself as a product manufacturer. In fact, the XOOM, and any good tablet, is a serious lifestyle enhancer. It keeps you organized; it keeps you entertained with movies and music. It shows you the memories of your lives with photos. It brings the Internet to you in a personal, interactive way. It is a brilliant, incredible device. But I don't get even a little bit of this from that press release. Do you?

Let's compare how Motorola positioned its XOOM product with the way another company, Apple, positioned the iPad. In the keynote speech that launched the iPad, CEO Steve Jobs used these words: amazing, wonderful, extraordinary, phenomenal, awesome, gorgeous, great, incredible, super high quality, terrific. There's even a three-minute YouTube video with more than one million views that shows nothing but Jobs using these words to describe his new product. The point? Jobs knows Apple's products are all about his customers' lifestyles. He is to the far right on the Manufacturer–Lifestyle Enhancer continuum and is actually training—teaching!—his customers, not to mention the media and analysts, how to talk about the iPad. See the difference? One company, which sees itself as a product manufacturer, talks about all the things its "potentially disruptive technology" can do. Another company, perceiving itself as a lifestyle enhancer, focuses on superlative ways its product will affect people. It's no accident that Apple is a media darling and a business superstar. Its marketing makes it so. And it all starts with the leadership's mindset: Apple is all about improving people's lives.

FIGURE 2.2

Shifting Your Mindset

How do you view yourself and your company?

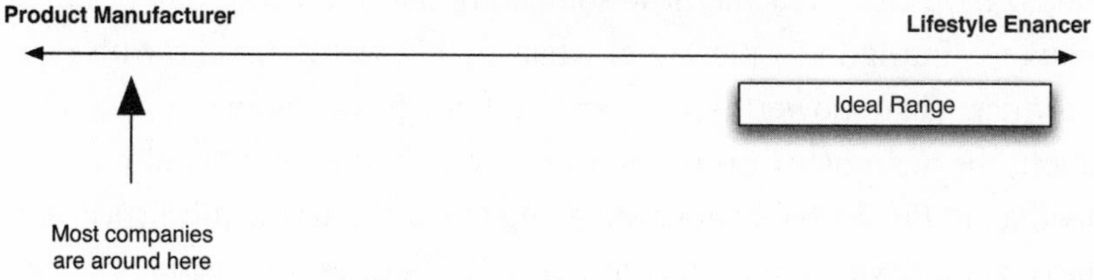

So, specifically, people who perceive their firms as product makers are:

- Focused on functions, not value
- Discussing technical specifications instead of life improvement
- Generally less effective marketers
- Challenged in creating consumer excitement
- Less aware of what consumers want from their devices because they usually spend less time finding out
- Often creating excellent devices that don't attain the customer bases they deserve

Conversely, individuals who perceive their consumer technology companies as lifestyle enhancers are:

- Almost always better marketers
- More effective at connecting with consumers and exciting them
- Focused on communicating how their products can help people
- Spending resources on developing effective language to describe their devices' value
- Talking about how people use their products instead of what their products can do

Here's a bit more on this important distinction: customer examples are always more powerful than features lists and technical specifications. If you can tell me how somebody like me uses your product, you're painting me a picture of what my life would be like with your product. That's powerful. Conversely, if you're asking me to read a list about the technology inside your product, I'm tuning it out almost immediately. I'm probably not even going to make it to the third spec, and most people will stop even before that. Tell stories, not features.

That's the difference between being in the product manufacturing business and the life improvement business. On the continuum between the two, most of you reading this right now work for or with companies that are a lot closer to the product manufacturing business. My challenge to you is to begin moving toward the other pole. Make incremental, small steps toward being in the lifestyle improvement business. Most of these steps must occur in your own mind—this is about how you perceive yourself and your company.

Shift Toward Marketing

Another continuum on which you must make progress is the distance between being a manufacturer and being a marketer. The majority of consumer technology companies are on the far left side of this continuum. As I've said before, in general, consumer electronics companies are great manufacturers but exceedingly poor marketers. This is mostly because many of the founders of successful technology firms are engineers themselves. They create the first versions of the products their company sells, and then bring in others to run the marketing part of the business. That means the highest executive direction at technology companies—even the largest, most successful ones like Microsoft, Samsung, and Sony—is set by people who are first and foremost engineers.

FIGURE 2.3

Shifting Your Mindset

How do you view yourself and your company?

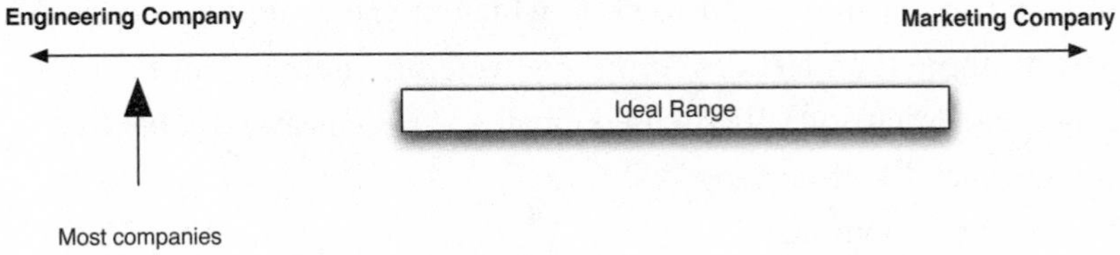

Let's look at Microsoft here.

In February 2005, when Microsoft was still widely acknowledged to be the leader in consumer technology, CEO Steve Ballmer, speaking about innovation at an event of the Cambridge Energy Research Association, said this:

> And so in a sense, the lifeblood of our business is that R&D spend. There's nothing that flows through a pipe or down a wire or anything else; we have to continuously create new innovation that lets people do something they didn't think they could do the day before so they get the newest version of a Windows or an Office or a new program, new application that we put in place. And so in a sense you could say all we have to live with is our innovation.

The lifeblood of our business is that [research and development] spend. In other words, the lifeblood of Microsoft is engineering. Not customers, not marketing, not communications, not branding. But engineering.

Of course, Microsoft has to be excellent at innovating. But it needs to be equally excellent at marketing. At exciting consumers. At creating energy in the marketplace for its products. Otherwise, they become just another company with decent products but bad marketing.

In mid-2010, Microsoft's vice president of communications, Frank X. Shaw, wrote a blog post that cited some amazing figures: in its first seven months of availability, the company had sold 150 million Windows® 7 licenses. That's 600,000 per day or one every seven seconds. In 2008, less than 10 percent of all netbooks in the United States ran Windows. In 2009, that number ballooned to 90 percent. Microsoft owned the netbook market. Microsoft's Xbox LIVE® subscription service had 23 million customers, which at the time, was nearly 50 percent more than Netflix! And there were 360 million Hotmail® users—that's Microsoft's Web-based email service—nearly double that of Google back then!

Sounds good, no?

Well, a few days later, San Jose State University business professor Randall Stross took a look at these numbers in the context of Microsoft's Wall Street performance. He said Microsoft's mid-2010 stock price was 55 percent below where it had been in January 2000. What a horrific statistic! A decade of work, a decade of providing and supporting Windows, the software used by more people than any other software in the world—and your stock price loses half of its value. By contrast, over the same period, Apple's stock price was up 829 percent. In the second quarter of 2010, Microsoft earned more profit than Apple and Google combined! Financial performance was solid. Excellent even. And yet, judging from the stock price—the most significant measure available—investors were punishing Microsoft.

But why?

Because despite its sales and profit success, despite the fact that it was selling Microsoft Windows licenses incredibly quickly, Microsoft created little to no energy among consumers. When Apple released a product like a new iPhone or iPad, it was on the front page of most newspapers and news Web sites in the country. It was on radio shows. It was at the water cooler at work. People buzzed. Similar things happened around Google's various releases, although to a lesser extent. Android™ devices create consumer energy. Google TV products were news. But Microsoft Windows 7? It was the company's biggest software release in years, but who do you know that got really excited about it? It can be somewhat shocking to financial minds, but consumer buzz has a rather pronounced effect on the stock performance of popular electronics makers. Buzz creates energy among the media (which then builds the buzz by covering it) and among mainstream consumers (who buy more product and generate even more buzz).

The irony is that it really was an exciting release. Modern, visually advanced, and far more secure than its predecessors, Windows 7 was arguably Microsoft's best work of the decade. But Steve Ballmer ran a company whose "lifeblood" was the "R&D spend." Admittedly, he wasn't focused on marketing the value of Windows 7. Nor was he focusing the company on communicating the many ways Windows could improve customers' lives. (In that 2005 speech, he also said this: "Some people tell you all they do is listen to their customers. Any innovator who tells you that is not an innovator who's going to succeed.")

It's not just listening, although Steve Ballmer certainly needs to listen to his customers more. More importantly, Microsoft needs to understand what their customers think about Windows and Microsoft Office. And I don't mean automatically collecting the reasons why a program crashed or why a computer needed to be restarted. I mean really understanding how people use, think about, and talk about Microsoft products. But because Microsoft doesn't have this information, it can't say the right things to consumers. Microsoft doesn't know what to say to consumers because Microsoft isn't asking its consumers how they use, think about, and talk about its products. It's what this book is about. Steve Ballmer and Microsoft need to move to the right of where they currently are on the Engineering–Marketing continuum.

Remember these continuums are about self-perception. The executives at Microsoft—and at the vast majority of technology manufacturers—need to recast themselves as marketer–engineers. I put *marketer* first in that pairing for a reason. Because most companies are to the far left of the continuum, directly under Engineering, they need to slide toward the middle of the range, and place a heavy emphasis on the marketing function of their business. Marketing is everything in our business. At the small manufacturer level, amazing products fail because not enough people know about them. At the large manufacturer level, great products fail because the company fails at creating consumer passion and energy.

To begin the process of creating evangelists, you must begin thinking of yourself as a marketer, and of your organization as a marketing company.

Shifting Toward Passionate Consumers

FIGURE 2.4

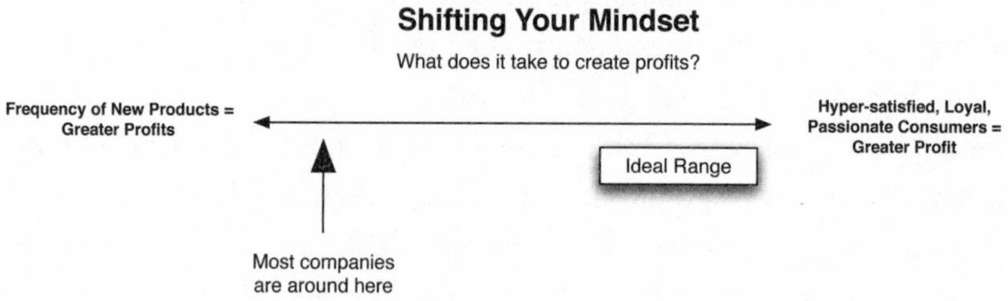

One of the biggest complaints consumers have about the technology industry is that too many new products are released. How many times have you heard someone say some variation of this: *I just bought this [insert any high-tech product here] three months ago, and there's already a newer model available?* There are many industry behaviors that upset the market—for example, poor product instructions, highly technical language, inept retail assistance—but too-frequent product releases are one of the biggest offenders.

The problem is that this behavior is deeply ingrained in the industry. Most consumer electronics executives believe that there is a direct correlation between the frequency of new products and the profitability of their company. I would argue that 90 percent of new models released onto the retail market—from televisions to computers to digital cameras to software—only incrementally improve on the preceding version. A 10 percent improvement by a new release over the previous model is a fairly dramatic improvement in our business. That's a major release. The reality is, the technology industry depends on new model numbers—new SKUs—to create new sales. (A lot of this, interestingly, has to do with the dichotomy discussed in the previous section: most tech makers see themselves as manufacturers, not marketers. As Microsoft's Ballmer said, innovation is the lifeblood. So, for many in the industry, the high frequency of new releases has a lot to do with its common innovate-or-die outlook.)

Ironically, the behavior of releasing an endless stream of products into the market has the opposite effect of what is intended: instead of piquing consumer interest, it piques consumer frustrations. Instead of creating a need for the latest and greatest among consumers, it creates resentment because consumers feel like their recent purchase is now out of date. I've heard people vow never to buy another product from a manufacturer again because their products were replaced so quickly.

So the final way I'm going to challenge you to shift your mindset is this: your frequency of new product releases does not increase your profits nearly as much as satisfied, loyal, and passionate consumers. They are, in fact, opposites, and inversely proportional. The more products you pour into the marketplace, the less loyal and passionate your customers become. This shift in mindset should lead to a shift in resources as well: from developing products to developing thrilled customers. The rest of the chapters in this book will tell you my approach to doing the latter. But the first step, and the most important one, is to shift how you think. Even if the shift is small and slow.

Shifting Your Approach to Strategy Formulation

Enough about you.

Let's talk about how you approach creating marketing strategy.

In the last chapter, I laid out how engineers are almost unknowingly leading marketing strategy at consumer electronics companies.

They develop the products. They educate the marketing department about the products' features and functions. And for many manufacturers, much of the language used at these sessions makes it into the final product messaging. Of course, your engineers are precisely the wrong people to be directing communications designed to convince the media and consumers about your products' excellence. Engineers spend their time making technology. Consumers spend their time using it.

Your marketing professionals spend much of their time kneading, crafting, shaping, and molding the features descriptions provided by the products' developers. They give you the clay to work with, only it's defective clay. It's ugly, difficult to work with, and it doesn't hold its form. And when you're finally done with the difficult work of turning this difficult clay into a finished piece, it's obvious to everyone early on that this is not a beautiful work. How could it be? It's clear that the raw material was bad. Your raw material—the product features, functions, branding, positioning, and language that you use—is bad. That's because, by default, it originates with your engineers. Your clay is bad. You need much better clay, and you get it from your consumers.

Shift to Consumers

The first shift in your approach to creating marketing strategy is to involve consumers in it. And not just a little bit but significantly and deeply. Gather consumer experiences, opinions, and advice at the very beginning of your marketing strategy development. The best way to do this is not focus groups or wide-reaching surveys. (These certainly have a purpose, but effective brand and positioning strategy is not one of them.) The best way to involve consumers in your strategy is through long-form qualitative interviews. I detail strategies and sample interviews for doing this in Chapter 5.

This idea of involving consumers early and often usually, understandably, meets with resistance among my clients. Engineering doesn't like it because I am advocating limiting their role to—gasp!—engineering. But nothing really changes for them if you are successful in executing this shift. They continue developing excellent products, and continue briefing the company in difficult-to-understand ways about them. The marketing department continues to attend these unveilings, and, to the extent that it is possible for human beings to understand engineers talking about products, digests as much of what they're presented as possible. It is at this point that my recommendation to involve consumers begins—after marketing is briefed by engineering but before the marketing department processes the technical presentations they attend about new products. Consumers should be involved to help create your products' name (yes, name!) and everything else that's critical to your products' success: branding, positioning, top features, key messaging, press releases, media pitches, packaging design, and documentation. All. Of. That.

This is where my clients tend to get a little uneasy, so I want to address the marketers for a moment: this shift in focus from your engineers' product details to your consumers' experiences and thoughts will not only make you far more effective (meaning, increased retail distribution, increased consumer sales, increased media coverage, all the increases you're trying to attain), but it will make your lives easier. You'll no longer need to struggle to translate what the product developers were trying to say into what may actually make sense to consumers. Rather, you'll have concrete, powerful experiences directly from your customers to use in formulating your strategy. It's a straight line to effective marketing, not a squiggly dotted one.

Let's compare the two approaches: the one that's in place at most consumer electronics companies today, and the one I'm proposing.

Here are eleven consequences of engineers setting the marketing tone inside your company (the default at most tech makers, even if they don't know it is so):

1. The language is highly technical.
2. The branding is confused.
3. There is little to no involvement of consumers.
4. The wrong features are emphasized, and powerful ones often go unmentioned.
5. The consequences are far-reaching—even the PR department's press releases are far less effective.

6. Therefore, there is less media coverage.
7. That means fewer consumers hear about your products.
8. Fewer consumers have the opportunity to get excited about your devices.
9. You sell fewer products.
10. There is less word-of-mouth buzz.
11. Even your packaging is rarely as helpful to the sale as it could be.

Conversely, here are eleven results of involving consumers at the beginning of and throughout the process of creating your marketing strategy:

1. The language is powerful—because it comes from the intended audience.
2. Branding is sharp and effective—again, because your customers tell you what works.
3. You know exactly which features are most valuable to your customers, and you emphasize them in your branding, positioning, communications, and media outreach.
4. Your executive team is better educated about how real people use your creations. They're more aware, and therefore much more effective.
5. You have deep insights about (a) what your consumers like about your products, (b) what they do with your product, and c) the perceived value that it brings them.
6. You use this information in shaping your media outreach, detailing specific consumer stories.
7. The media loves this, and I guarantee that you'll generate far more coverage as a result.
8. More consumers will hear about your products.
9. More consumers will have an opportunity to be passionate about your products.

10. There will be a dramatic increase in word-of-mouth buzz.
11. Sales will be significantly higher with this approach. (How could they not be?)

There's one point about this shift that contrasts with the others: a small step here is not enough. This needs to be a complete shift—a change. Instead of engineers establishing the language used, it should be consumers. Remember, that language sets the tone for all your marketing, branding, and media outreach, and ultimately determines what consumers hear about your products and your company. You should develop that strategy with your consumers. Let the engineers do what they're good at, but don't let their language leave the confines of your corporate offices.

This shift, therefore, looks more like this:

FIGURE 2.5

Shifting Your Approach to Strategy Formulation

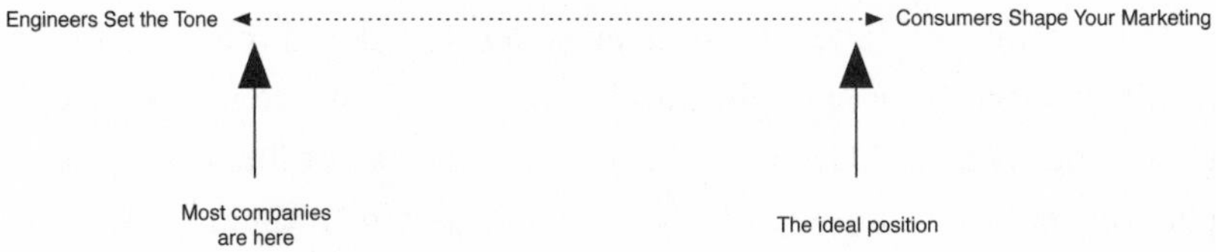

Shift Toward Involving Your PR Department Early

Later in this book—also earlier!—I detail the real problems caused by public relations departments and agencies for consumer technology makers. PR people, particularly those who pitch the media, are often young and ineffective. Journalists literally wonder aloud how such sophisticated companies can put so much of their company's success into the hands of such unsophisticated, low-level employees. Chapter 9 covers in depth the problems caused by your public relations professionals and prescribes solutions.

But this section, this next shift in your approach to formulating marketing strategy, involves making far better use of your public relations teams. At most companies I've worked with as a consultant and before that as a journalist, public relations is the last to be let in on outbound communications strategy but the first to distribute it to the media. That puts your PR people in the unique and valuable position of being among the first people in your company to get feedback about how your strategy is working. In fact, on a day-to-day basis, your public relations professionals get more reaction about your branding, positioning, and messaging than anyone else in the marketing function.

The problem is, PR is the tail being wagged by the marketing dog. (The head of the dog is engineering.) Generally, your PR department receives instructions and executes them. Engineering develops the products and sets the course for what will be emphasized and how. Marketing molds what engineering gives them into a strategy: it develops the branding approach, the product story; identifies the heroes; crafts the messages, the language, the platforms from which everything will be distributed; and incorporates an advertising and media strategy into the larger plan. For most companies, this process takes weeks, if not months, for each product.

It is only then, after the strategy is developed and the direction is firmly set, that PR is brought into the process: Here are the products. Here's the message. Get it to the media. In most companies, public relations executives execute orders handed down to them. This is all wrong. As the group of people who are among the first to distribute your carefully crafted messaging, and the first to get reaction and feedback on it, public relations must be much more involved in your strategy creation process. And I don't mean involving the vice president of public relations or the people who run communications in North America and Europe. I'm talking about everyone from communications specialists to media relations managers, the front-line folks.

These people who distribute your message and fight for it on the battlefield of rude, rushed, unresponsive media should be brought into the earliest stages of your marketing planning. They know things your executives do not. Even though your media relations people may be young, they have experience relating to the media. They have instincts about what will and won't work. They'll be able to tell you, for example, that megahertz and megabytes are now meaningless to media. But an interesting consumer story, a memorable experience, is worth its weight in gold. They know this because they've had thousands of pitches declined, and also a few that have been accepted. Why would you not want to leverage this knowledge?

There are considerable benefits to this approach:

- Knowledge and experience that is unique to front-line public relations professionals is contributed to product marketing strategy.
- This brings a new real-world realism to the planning stages.
- Here's the most powerful benefit of all: you'll develop a more effective branding and positioning strategy for your products. Messaging will be more powerful. Language will be stronger. That is your media team's domain!
- Your PR professionals, who often feel interchangeable (because they often are, burning out one after another, from endless press release distribution, follow-ups, and rejections), will feel valuable and involved.
- As such, because they were involved with the development of the plan, they'll be more effective at executing it.
- The constant rejection that is the currency of their domain won't sting as much. They'll become more resilient.
- They'll be more inclined to communicate back to leadership about the media and outside reactions to the content they're distributing. This new information will allow you to make in-game adjustments. It's information you may not have been privy to in the past.

If you're dubious or hesitant (and that's a normal reaction to suggested changes, but you're reading this book for a reason), ask yourself this: What can it hurt? It's pretty much impossible that involving your front-line PR professionals early in the marketing planning phase can hurt. It can only help. What can you lose by trying?

Here's what this shift looks like—it's another one that is black or white. You must move from the left, where you probably are now, to the right, which is the desired destination.

FIGURE 2.6

Shifting Your Approach to Strategy Formulation

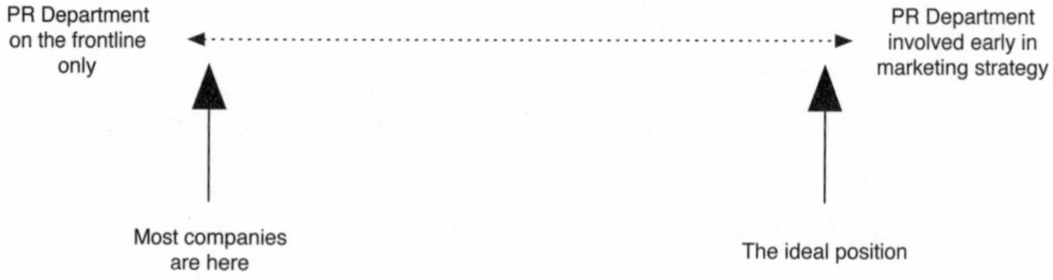

Additional Resource

Go to my Web site, TechnologyTailor.com, for fifty questions to ask your staff to identify and understand your internal corporate mindset on these shifts. Click the image of the book cover to find this free document and other support resources.

Shifting Your Customers' Perceptions

The final shift that needs to be enacted is in the minds of your customers. Of the three major changes this chapter discusses—changing your mindset, changing your approach to formulating strategy, and this final one, changing your consumers' perceptions—this is the only "outcome shift." The first two changes, if executed effectively and correctly, will lead to this critical change.

Also, unlike the shifts discussed earlier in this chapter, you do not control this shift directly. You can decide to change how you view yourself and your company. Assuming your position is senior enough, you can decide (or at the very least, suggest) how your company goes about creating marketing strategy. But you can only influence your customers' mindset. You can enact strategies and execute techniques designed to change how consumers think about you—but ultimately, whether the shift in perception actually occurs is up to your customers, not you.

That said, you can do an awful lot to help consumers change how they think about your company and your products. In fact, the process laid out in this book is in many ways designed to change how consumers think about you. In this section, I want to lay out how your market sees you today, and what the desired perception is. This section will serve to mark the "you are here" position on the map, and identify the ultimate destination. The turn-by-turn directions (spoken street names and all!) to get you from here to there come in the chapters that follow.

Statements of Fact

Before laying out how consumers view technology, I want to emphasize some statements of fact. Some of these assumptions have already been laid out, and all of them are likely to be repeated in this book. I repeat them because understanding them is vital to improving your marketing.

- Most technology from name-brand makers on the mainstream consumer market is functionally good. In other words, if your products have made it to Best Buy or Amazon's electronics store, they almost certainly do what you say they do. I know from my personal voracious shopping habit (my wife might call what I have a *shopping problem*), as well as these simple realities the products have to be good in order to survive in today's hypercompetitive market. They have to be good to get retail distribution. They have to be good because we live in an age when people take their dissatisfaction to the Internet. So, you can disagree with me on this, but most devices from well-known manufacturers at major retail work very well—most of the time. I'll have more on product excellence in Chapter 4.

- How consumers perceive your technology has nothing to do with how good your technology is. Rather, the market's perception is a function of how effective your marketing is—how well you can convince them that your products are excellent.
- Not only can customers' perceptions of your products be influenced—they *must* be influenced. If you don't do everything possible to convince as many people as possible that they need your devices, you're doing consumers—not to mention all the hardworking colleagues at your company—a disservice. People deserve to know about your products. And you owe it to them to do everything in your power to educate them.

How Consumers Perceive Technology

Most consumers perceive technology as falling into one of three categories: commodities, special, and singular. Here's what this looks like:

FIGURE 2.7

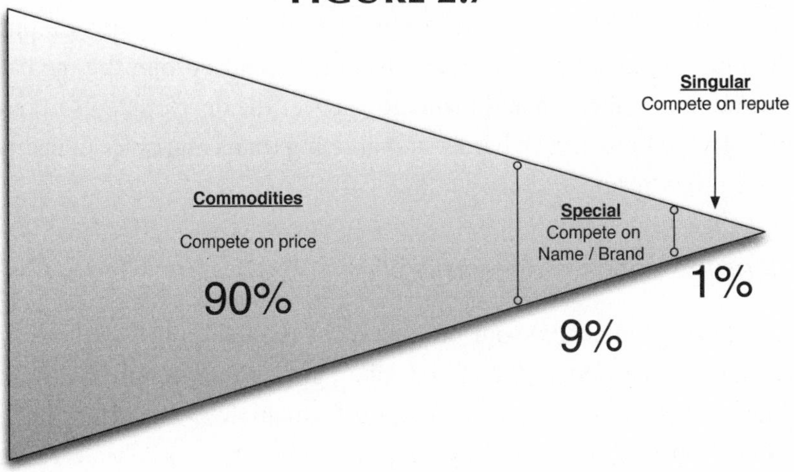

Commodities

Nine out of ten consumer electronics products—hardware, software, and Internet sites and services—are perceived as interchangeable commodities by consumers. If you make high-definition televisions, your TV is seen by the public as very much like Samsung's. Or LG's. Or even Sony's. (Years ago, Sony would sell televisions simply because its name was on them. Sony meant quality. Excellence. In 2010, upstart Vizio was outselling Sony in the television category.) If you make digital cameras, your point-and-shoot is very much like Kodak's. Or Canon's. Or Nikon's. Your printer is very much like the other printers on the market. So is your personal computer. Product excellence is expected, and in most cases, delivered. Product excellence is no longer considered special or even interesting. It is simply assumed.

This is a rather huge obstacle to overcome for manufacturers in our industry and it's an obstacle that's unique to our industry. The auto industry doesn't have to deal with this. High-end cars like Mercedes and BMWs are certainly not seen as commodities. In the clothing category, people have favorite brands that fit them better than others. But you'll rarely hear a consumer say, *I only buy Samsung smartphones*. I can't think of another business that has so many excellent companies making so many terrific products—all of which are seen as nearly identical and interchangeable with the competition. It means that, despite the intense interest in consumer electronics, and despite the media's natural involvement in and mandate to cover the developments in our industry, you must work harder at marketing than companies in nearly every other business category.

Characteristics of Commodities

Consumers don't know your product name. Can you think of the various names that Kodak, Canon, or Nikon give to their point-and-shoot digital cameras (if you don't own one)? Me neither.

Consumers don't know your product number. Go ahead: name some product numbers from Nokia. Or Panasonic televisions. Consumers don't go to the store—online or offline—looking specifically for your product. They need to do a lot of research first. They need to be convinced to buy your device by professional reviews and consumer reviews.

Consumers delay purchasing commodities but act much faster with special and singular products (the next two categories of your customers' product perception). Commodities stall people. Special and singular items catalyze the buying process.

People are less excited when they finally do buy a commodity. Who do you think is the more energized consumer, the iPhone customer or the Nokia/Samsung/LG customer? As a result, customers talk to friends and family much less about your products after the purchase. Recommendations are less frequent. Word-of-mouth buzz is nearly nonexistent.

For many other industries, such a commodity culture would be death but not in consumer electronics because of the intense public interest in technology. The market's interest overcomes the antipathy created by a commodity culture. So companies can make commodities, distribute them, sell them, and still claim success. Unfortunately, and obviously, you could be so much more successful. If consumers saw your products as special (the second category of consumer perception, detailed next), you'd be playing at a completely different level than the commodity competition.

Why Consumer Technology Products Are Seen as Commodities

Here are the main reasons consumers perceive most products as commodities:

- Manufacturers oversaturate the market with products. Too many companies release too many new products that offer just minor, incremental improvements over the previous version. This not only frustrates consumers but multiplies the number of products that are nearly identical to one another. Frequent new models mean new revenue for you in the short term, but in the long term they actually contribute to commoditizing your product lines. A simple decrease in the frequency of product updates would go a long way here. Look at Apple, which has achieved the most desired consumer perception—people think Apple creates singular products. Apple updates its product lines once a year, no more. It updates different lines at different times of the year, so as to maintain a constant media presence, but the frequency per product is annual. If once a year is enough for the most successful company in consumer electronics, it should be enough for you.
- Intense competition has led to a narrowing in technical specifications. Products from different companies are very similar. Everyone sees what works, and does it, too. Why not? It's good business. But there's more to this, given that many companies are using the same suppliers and overseas manufacturing plants. Many of the televisions from most of the popular brands are made in the same factories. So not only are the products perceived as being very similar, they truly are identical on the inside.

- In many categories, the innovation ceiling has been reached. In the modern consumer electronics era, this happened first in personal computers. Remember, back in the mid-1990s? Things got to a point where it didn't matter how much the megahertz were increased or how much RAM there was. Consumers could not perceive actual performance improvements. Later, the innovation ceiling was reached with digital cameras. Consumers couldn't care less if the camera had eight megapixels or twelve because there was no difference in picture quality or cropping capabilities. As I'm writing this book, I would argue that we've already seen most of the improvements we're going to get in high-definition televisions (3-D TVs notwithstanding, and I'm not convinced they'll enjoy nearly the mainstream consumption that flat-panel HDTVs enjoy). I would also say that most of the innovation we're going to see in smartphones has already occurred. We have keyboards, still cameras, video cameras, huge internal storage, movies (buy or rent!), music (yours or streaming), productivity, wildly useful app stores, and countless content developers. What's left to innovate here?
- The marketing is all the same, which is to say, poor. Sometimes, it's similarly embarrassing. Companies are too focused on the technical aspects of their devices, and not enough on the life-improvement aspects. As a result, all of the conversations about these devices are too technical. Marketers focus too much time and energy on Internet marketing, and particularly on social media, which is largely ineffective for convincing consumers that one company's high-technology device is better than the competition's.

Bottom line, this is a marketing problem. There is nothing you can do about the maturity of the categories you're in. There's little you can do about intense competition. You can release fewer products, but your competitors likely won't, so that's not a problem you can do much about either. But your marketing? That is within your control. What you say about your products is up to you. Where you say it is up to you. How you structure your message and language is up to you. You can choose to make your marketing better, and then you can choose exactly how you will go about making it better. That's a pretty powerful position to be in.

"They Don't Market Like They Used To"

"There are a variety of reasons for the lack of mainstream evangelists for digital cameras: the camera space has become commoditized, and now they're all fighting on megapixels. Consumers see these things as roughly comparable. Also, it's partly driven by the fact that camera manufacturers continue to focus on technical specification. Ten years ago, Kodak stood alone as the warm brand among cameras. It was the family favorite, the mom favorite. I think today they have suffered the general trend in the industry of commoditization. They don't market like they used to."

—Jef Holove, CEO of Basis, the wrist-wearable connected heart and health monitor; former CEO of Eye-Fi, makers of the market-leading wireless memory card

CONTINUED ON FOLLOWING PAGE . . .

CONTINUED . . .

Alex's Analysis: Kodak has tried to focus on lifestyle and its value to consumers' lives more than any other camera manufacturer during the digital camera revolution. This is both an accomplishment and an indictment. They deserve credit for talking about moms—typically, the home's photographer-in-chief—but they give up on those messages too quickly. Like most manufacturers, these lifestyle messages aren't consistently leveraged. Too often and too quickly, Kodak has been sucked back into the "spec wars" with its competition. My sense is the internal feeling is, *Let's talk to moms, but we have to compete with other manufacturers, so we have to compare our technology to theirs.* That's fine, make your tech specs available for those who want to dig deeper and find them. But—and this goes for anybody who has anything to do with a consumer technology company—focus all of your outgoing communication on how you will improve people's lives. Kodak has gained traction and results with that when they leveraged those messages, but they got away from them too quickly.

For a dramatic example of how ingrained the commoditization of consumer electronics is, look no further than one of the hottest battlefields in the industry—smartphones. Consumers love smartphones, right? Between 2008 and 2010, millions of people traded in their "features" phones—the kind that don't have app stores and advanced operating systems—for smartphones. It's one of the highest-growth categories in all of consumer electronics. Many companies, from wireless carriers to manufacturers to software companies, are investing aggressively in the smartphone category.

That, unfortunately, is precisely the problem.

There is one iPhone, maybe two—counting the immediately previous version that remains on the market before Apple phases it out. But at the end of 2010, there were at least thirty Android phones on the U.S. market. Consumers know what the choice is when it's time to buy an iPhone: the latest model, which most people choose, or the last model, which is significantly more affordable. That's it. Both feature hardware and software made and carefully controlled by Apple. Because of this, people know what to expect. They take comfort in the fact their iPhone will be exactly like the one they just saw being used at the airport or on the train.

On the Android operating system side, there are countless options, most of which are very similar. At the time of this writing, Samsung alone makes six Android devices. All have touchscreens between 3.4 inches and 4 inches wide. All have cameras. All have speakerphones. All are basically nearly identical in how they look and how they function. So which one do people choose?

Before we dig into that question, let's look at Motorola's Droid Android device, which launched the first popular Android device with incredible success among consumers and media. Back then, the choice was easy. If you wanted an Android smartphone, you got yourself a Droid. Today, Motorola alone sells more than ten Android models.

Of course, I realize that these various devices are made for, and sold by, different wireless carriers. But compare this commodity strategy to Apple's single device strategy. For years, the iPhone was sold exclusively by AT&T. Then, in early 2011, it became available from Verizon Wireless. Did Apple change the name for Verizon Wireless? Of course not; people wanted the iPhone, regardless of the service provider. Why in the world would Apple change the name? It's crazy for these devices to have different names when they are essentially functionally the same, regardless of the fact that PR departments emphasize different features for each of the devices. These are all Android phones. They bring the same set of features to consumers. Why do you take steps to confuse consumers, which undermines their ability to reference your product, talk about it to their peers, and, ultimately, to build your brand? Your own employees can barely keep all these models straight. Why do you insist on hanging this burden around your customers?

I have the answer to this question, but you won't like it. You flood the marketplace with new devices because they are a new revenue stream for you. This is true for the entire consumer electronics industry—from televisions to computers to cameras. New product models imply innovation (even if only one or two functionalities out of hundreds are improved in successive models). You are competing. You do it because everyone else in the industry is doing it. You do it to keep pace. You do it because it's what retailers expect at this point; after all, you've trained them to expect this.

Here's the huge problem with all this: you are commoditizing yourself, your product category, and the entire industry. Looking at our Android examples, you have taken an immensely popular technology and, by choice, commoditized it. By producing far too many options, you've weakened every manufacturer that makes these phones. You have created the Mac versus Windows issue all over again.

Remember Mac versus Windows? When there were hundreds of Windows-based computers from countless manufacturers? All of them had to compete against Apple, which made a few Mac computers. Even though Windows PCs vastly outsold Macs, it was very difficult, if not impossible, to build much brand loyalty in this category. Consumers couldn't get excited about Windows PCs—even though every one of them was using such a PC—because there was never a single PC they could focus their thoughts on. Hewlett-Packard's computer was just like Dell's, which was just like Gateway's, which, in turn, was just like e-Machines'. In the end, few people cared about what company made their computer because they were all the same. This is an impossible environment in which to build consumer evangelists.

And when Apple lambasted Microsoft Windows computers in those "I'm a Mac" commercials for years, this arrangement made it convenient for them to hit all of the Windows PC makers at once. "I'm a PC" was code for HP, Dell, Gateway, Sony, Toshiba, IBM, and all the others. This commoditization made it easy for Apple, which makes computers perceived as singular, to group and attack the commodity computers all at once.

You created that environment. And you're creating it—as if by force of habit—again in the Android smartphone space. And smartphones are a much more intimate device category than computers. They're with us when we're away from our homes and our loved ones. People are passionate about their smartphones. And already, we're starting to see consumers who couldn't care less about who makes their Android device. What matters is that they get an Android device. The manufacturer is irrelevant.

When You Make Commodities, All You Have Is Price

When you make products that are perceived as commodities, you only have one variable on which to compete: price. Brand name doesn't matter—consumers don't care. Product quality doesn't matter—most technology on the mainstream market is of high quality. Your warranty doesn't matter—it's probably the same as everyone else's. So what's left? Only price.

It's a terrible position to be in, but in consumer electronics, most companies are in it. So, at least, you have all your competition for company. But this is why how you price is so critical. If your price is too high, people won't buy your products because they have plenty of options that cost less. If your price is too low, they'll wonder what the catch is. So all you really have to separate yourself is a small range within which to price your products and sales and promotions. That's it.

It's a terrible place to be, isn't it? Want to change things? All you have to do is apply the steps in this book.

Special Products

Consumers think of only about one product in ten as special. Through excellent marketing, these products have broken away from the engulfing commodities pack. Here are the characteristics of special products:

- Special products are known to consumers by name.
- People know what these products do—their features, their functionality.

- People have heard about these devices from their friends, family, and colleagues. They've listened to stories about these devices.
- Consumers generally speak warmly and positively about these products.
- These products have attained "mindshare" among their market. They are elevated above the competitive fracas in consumers' minds.
- Special products are discussed in major print and broadcast media.
- Special products have attained a level of consumer trust that commodities do not enjoy.
- People aspire to own special products. (Think about what a huge advantage this is.)
- People are intrigued by these devices, curious about what it would be like to have them, and make efforts to attain them.

What Is and Is Not Seen as a Special Product

Blackberry® smartphones are perceived as special products. They broke away from the smartphone pack long ago. People know what a Blackberry is. The consensus is that they're great for email, dependable, tough under hard use, and made for businesspeople. Although not as sexy as other smartphones, a Blackberry can be relied upon. Blackberry smartphones work. The intended audience knows this. It's why people keep using and buying Blackberry smartphones in the face of temptations from sexier alternatives.

Nokia phones are not seen as special by consumers. They used to be, as one of the first smartphone makers. But Nokia's marketing became ineffective, and as a result of decreasing sales, innovation stalled as well. The frequency of new devices dropped significantly, and consumers don't see the older models on the market as compelling. The same can be said for LG, which makes phones that most people simply buy because they are an option at their wireless carrier's store. That's true for Sony-Ericsson, too.

Consumers see Android-based smartphones as special. They're unique and strong competition to the iPhone. Android devices enjoy buzz in the media. A variety of manufacturers and carriers advertise them constantly. Android has become a part of the social conversation. People post on Facebook about how much they're enjoying their new Android device. Interestingly, it is precisely because of their sheer quantities that Android devices will never achieve singular status among consumers. There's only one iPhone at a time. It's singular. (More on this in the next section.) But which Android device do you promote to singular status? Early on in the Android life cycle, Motorola's Droid looked like it was headed there, but it was soon joined by more than twenty additional Android phones.

The Nintendo Wii® is seen as a special product by consumers. People know the Wii. They know what it does, how it works, and by now, most people have either played a Wii system or been in the room while it was being used. People see television news segments about nursing home residents taking part in a virtual bowling tournament.

The Xbox 360 on the other hand, although well known, is not seen as a special product. Most mainstream consumers couldn't tell you one thing that makes the Xbox special. It's a video game system that their kids play. But that's it. Details are not widely known. Media buzz is not widespread. The Xbox is perceived as a commodity.

All HDTVs are perceived as commodities. Not one company has broken out of that crowded, profitable category to rise above the noise in consumers' minds. Vizio is the closest thing that comes to my mind, thanks to strong marketing, but its televisions are not perceived as being any more special today than Sony's or Samsung's.

All point-and-shoot digital cameras are perceived as commodities. So are all video cameras. There was a time when the Flip digital camcorder was widely seen by consumers as a special product, but powerful HD video cameras built into smartphones ended that. Once phones started shipping with excellent camcorders built in, consumers saw the Flip as just another product to buy and carry.

Online, Google is seen as special but not singular. On the Internet, this is a huge achievement because of the vast options that are available. Amazon is seen as special by consumers, in the top 5 to 10 percent of sites where people are comfortable spending money online. This is also a massive success for an e-commerce company. Both companies have a difficult path to singular status because, even though both are ubiquitous in many consumers' lives, a Web site rarely enjoys consumer word-of-mouth recommendations.

Amazon, however, has attained singular status for its main product. And there is one Web site that has attained singular status in consumers' minds.

Singular Products

Consumers perceive only one in 100 products as singular. Singular products are a cultural phenomenon. They are far more than a piece of high technology—they become ingrained into the social fabric of day-to-day life. They are not only hugely popular, but they define a time period. Most of the population has heard of singular products, and know what they do. Singular products may have a lot of competition, but they dominate their category, both in terms of sales and in marketing and public relations.

One of the surest indicators of a singular product is an intensely loyal consumer following that almost borders on the religious. It's why I call these people evangelists. They'll tell anyone who will listen about how wonderful these products are. Consumer evangelists are profiled in detail in Chapter 6. Attaining evangelist consumers should be the goal of any consumer product company. Let me be clear: consumer evangelists create singular products by talking about products and elevating their status. Eventually, once evangelists tip a product into the singular realm, new consumers are attracted by all of the attention, and new evangelists are created. This is a self-fulfilling prophesy:

FIGURE 2.8

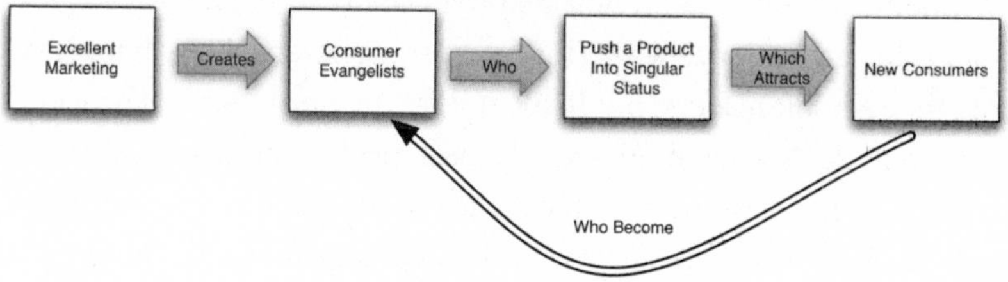

Therefore, a key difference between special products and singular products is that singular products enjoy consumer evangelists, but special products do not. Once more, this is because mainstream consumer evangelists elevate a product into singular status.

What Singular Products Have in Common

In order for a product to achieve singular status, it must be functionally excellent—step one in technology marketing success.

None of them were first to the market in their category. There were computers before the Mac. There were many smartphones before the iPhone. Likewise, there were countless MP3 players before the iPod. And there were a number of tablets on the market before the iPad. The Kindle was not the first e-book reader. And you could rent videos before Netflix appeared on the scene.

Instead of being first, these products *perfected* their respective categories. By consensus, they're the best product in each of their categories. Each company unleashed spectacularly effective marketing, much of which I talk about in this book.

As each company developed consumer evangelists for its product, their customers took over their marketing and messaging. For a consumer, there is no more effective marketing than having a friend or colleague who can't stop gushing about their new product.

When the Kindle e-book reader first came out, I spoke to hundreds of people who owned one on my radio show (it was a call-in talk show, and I covered the e-book readers a lot!). Every single one of them loved their Kindle, to the point where they were motivated to pick up the phone and tell a radio host—and all of my listeners!—about how wonderful their Kindle was. This is consumer evangelism. Sure, there are other e-book readers, but the Kindle is the one to have. The Kindle is the one that's known. You rarely hear people talking about Sony's e-reader, even though it's an excellent product, and it was the first e-book reader on the market with the very same screen technology as the Kindle. That's because Sony's book reader is a commodity, but the Kindle is a singular product, on the other end of the continuum.

It's because this is a singular product, defining not only the category, not only the entire technology industry, but the time period we are living in. If you are involved with a consumer technology company, your only goal for that business should be to develop singular products. You do this by creating terrific technology and catapulting it into the world with sensational marketing that—and this is the key—needs to develop consumer evangelists. Consumer evangelists will take your products to singular status.

Chapter Summary

Success begins with a series of mindset shifts:

- Think about yourself and your company as a lifestyle enhancer, not a product manufacturer.
- Become a marketing company instead of an engineering company.
- Work toward more loyal consumers, not more product releases.
- Shift toward involving your consumers much earlier in your marketing formulation.
- Shift your consumers' perceptions. They think of most products as commodities. Take steps to make them think of your devices as special or singular.

three

A Revolutionary System for Creating Consumer Electronics Evangelists

This chapter is an introduction to my system for creating mainstream consumer electronics evangelists. It's a big-picture, 35,000-foot view of how to create those loyal, energetic, and passionate customers.

FIGURE 3.1

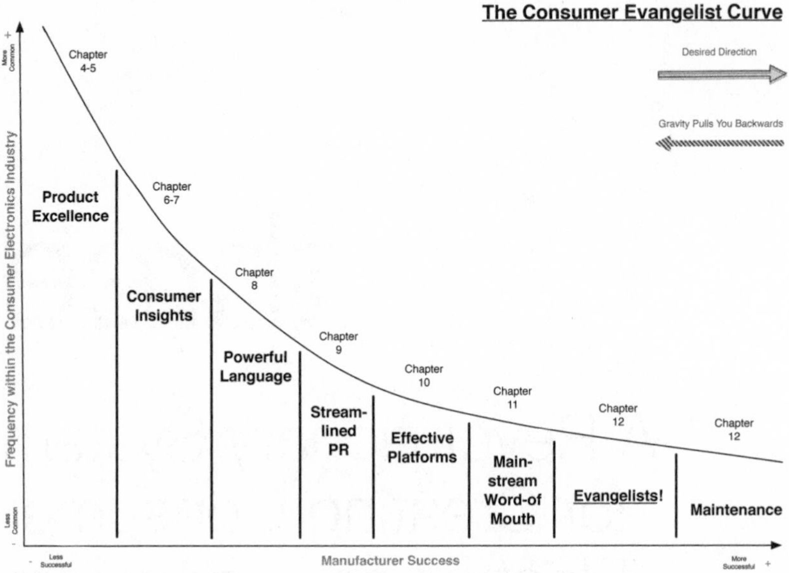

This is what the process looks like. Each step above is an achievement, a goal to attain. The process moves from left to right, in order. First, you have to get the product right—from functional excellence to ease of use, from appropriate pricing to a strong product name (all of which I cover in Chapters 4 and 5). Next, you have to have deep insights about your consumers: you need to know what they want from your products, how they want to use them, and what they think about your devices (Chapters 6 and 7). Next comes perfecting your language (Chapter 8). That's followed by powerful communication, public relations, media interaction, and effective platforms (Chapters 9 and 10). Finally, once you attain mainstream consumers, you must take steps to facilitate their buzz building, and allow them to generate their word-of-mouth recommendations (Chapter 11), and then, if all goes right, you arrive at consumer evangelists (Chapter 12).

Many companies have attained the early steps in my system—that's the Y-axis: frequency of achievement within the industry. As the system moves right, there are fewer and fewer companies on the model. The farther to the right you get, the more successful you will be with consumers (that's the X-axis), and the more elite your company becomes.

Progress Must Be Chronological

For optimal results, each step must be attained and maintained before moving on to the next step.

So, although it's possible to attain mainstream consumers before developing powerful and effective language (an earlier step on the model), it's much more difficult to maintain that position over the long term. You can see this by looking at Microsoft, which is struggling to stay relevant with desktop PC software while the rest of the high-technology industry moves to Web-based applications and cloud computing. Further, unless you attain each step in order, it's almost impossible to progress to the ultimate conclusion of the model: developing consumer evangelists. How can Microsoft create passionate consumers, for example, when they aren't using powerful language to create unquestionable perceived value for their consumers? Microsoft is stuck at the mainstream consumer stage.

Gravity Pushes Backward

You must maintain your position at each level. When you attain a certain level in this business, you must continue working on the right things simply to stay there. You must constantly innovate, communicate, brand, and position yourself to maintain your position on this model—and in consumers' minds. Gravity pushes backward. That is, if you stop marketing or if you stop communicating, you will quickly lose the market position you worked so hard to achieve. This is simply how the world works. Look at Palm, Inc., which once made the most popular smartphone on the planet, the Treo™. Do you remember how people used to love the Treo? In 2003, the Palm Treo 300 and 600 were all the rage in wireless phones. On the model above, Palm had attained the Word-of-Mouth level, and all the ones preceding it. Then, sometime in the middle of the decade, Palm stopped taking advantage of its hard-earned position in consumers' hearts and minds, and simply stopped talking to people. Palm ceased communication with their customers. The rest is a consumer electronics tragedy we've seen before but perhaps never so dramatically: consumers moved on to more interesting options from companies who were talking to them. Palm's revenue fell dramatically; as such, it couldn't invest as significantly in new product innovation, which meant it lagged even further behind the likes of Apple, Research in Motion, and the various Android makers. And then, when it could no longer survive, it was purchased by Hewlett-Packard for a small fraction of what it was once worth. And it all hinged on a sudden cessation of communication. You need to keep innovating and executing effective marketing to maintain your position with consumers.

Let's take a brief look at the major areas of the system.

Product Excellence (Chapters 4 and 5)

Everything begins with a terrific product. If your product isn't excellent, there is no point in doing anything else. This used to be more of a problem, but as I've said before (and I will repeat it again in this book), product engineering is not your problem. Your devices, if available on the mainstream market, are usually good. Many of your products are excellent. Still, it's worth identifying specifically how consumer electronics must excel in order to stand a chance of developing customer evangelists.

Products must be functionally excellent: The product must do what you say it does. People must feel like they are getting what was promised. But the most successful consumer electronics products and services—the ones that enjoy consumer evangelists—have these additional intangibles: they exceed people's expectations consistently, their additional functionality is a surprise, and they connect people to something that was missing before the product or service came into their lives.

Products must be easy to use and intuitive: The customer experience must be smooth. Setup must be easy and fast. Technical maintenance should be nearly nonexistent after an initial setup. Customers should be able to find their way around the product without too much help from a manual. If people have to dig in your manual or worse, deal with your tech support, you have work to do in this area. The worst thing that can happen in this category is that people end up resorting to Google to find an answer to their problems. At that point, you lose control of the customer experience and people begin to be influenced by other, usually unhappy, customers having the same issues.

Products should have a feel-good factor (FGF): The technologies that generate the most passionate consumer following are able to create a warm-and-fuzzy feeling for their customers. Consider Apple's products. People will tell you that it just feels good to use a Mac (they don't say this about Windows computers) or an iPhone (they don't say this about Nokia phones). People are constantly talking about what a pleasure it is to read on their Amazon Kindle e-reader (but you don't hear this about Sony's e-reader). People love the Netflix service, and all the content they get access to for about $8 per month. And they talk about it! (But you almost never hear people talking about how great they feel using Blockbuster's subscription service.) Aim for the FGF.

Products must be appropriately priced: This is a big one, and getting this right is critical to your product's success. Consumers have an expectation of how much various products should cost. This is established by a combination of the market, their experiences, and their perceptions. Price your product too high, and you lose people immediately to the competition. Price your device too low, and people wonder what the catch is. Avoid unnecessary issues by pricing your products within people's expectations. I call this the Consumer Pricing Expectations Range, and I cover it in depth in the next chapter.

Finally, products must be widely available at retail: People should be able to find your devices in the first place they check, whether it's online or in a physical store.

Deep Insights About Your Consumers (Chapters 6 and 7)

This is one of the key steps on your path to consumer electronics evangelists. In our wildly competitive business, where most people see your products as commodities, you must have a deep, rich, detailed understanding of your consumers. Focus groups are not enough here (although they can generate reasonably helpful information). You don't need more quantitative information. Rather, I am suggesting conducting extended qualitative interviews with your customers to understand how they think, perceive, use, and talk about your products.

Three of the five products with a critical mass of consumer evangelists are made by Apple, which boasts a great competitive advantage over the competition. That advantage is Steve Jobs. He has an incredible instinct for creating products that consumers will love. In fact, he has famously insisted that it's not the consumer's job to know what he wants. Jobs publicly states that Apple never does consumer research. That's because Apple has Jobs. And since your company does not, you'll have to do the next best thing and uncover deep insights from your customers by interviewing them.

I've said several times that you must aim directly at the mainstream, and avoid highly technical early adopters. You'll find that techie early adopters actually block the path to mainstream consumers. That's because everything is different for highly technical adopters. They read specialized message boards. They communicate in technical terms. The reasons they purchase technology are different from those of mainstream consumers. To communicate with early adopters, you'll have to create language and use platforms that won't work with more typical consumers. That means you'll need to develop a whole new set of messages and master an entirely different set of platforms to get at the mainstream. Although early adopters may ultimately play a role in your product's success, there is no guarantee that success with them will lead to success with your wider audience. Not only that, but given all this, I would argue that success with the early adopters often leads to failure with mainstream consumers. High-tech early adopters indirectly *block* your path to the mainstream. So shift your aim slightly, from highly technical early adopters to mainstream buyers. Your earliest customers should be the market you want to end up in. This way, there is no transition from early adopters to mainstream consumers. In my systems, your early adopters *are* mainstream consumers.

Understand what your consumers want from your style of product. If your company makes phone accessories, for example, do you know, in specifics, what customers expect from your products? What life improvements are they looking for when considering your device? Even if you think you know, it has been my experience that a majority of my clients—some of the biggest and best-regarded consumer technology makers in the world, with marketing budgets in the tens and hundreds of millions—don't know what their customers expect from their products. If they don't know, it is safe to assume that you probably don't either. This is nothing to be defensive or upset about. Rather, it's a massive opportunity to learn what your customers want, and integrate it into your marketing and communications.

Understand exactly how consumers use your product. What features are used most? Least? Who uses the product in a typical household? Which features are used most? Which ones are underused? Why? Are consumers using your device more than they thought (are they pleasantly surprised)? Or are they using it less than they expected (do they feel let down by your product)?

Understand how consumers think about your products. You have to know how people think about your style of product (that is, smartphones, TVs, cameras, etc.) and, critically, how they think about your products. It's stunning to say this, but nine out of ten manufacturers I work with do not have sufficient insight into their customers' thought processes. Why? Because so few companies conduct in-depth qualitative interviews with their customers. They see them as being too time-consuming and too expensive. The depressing irony is that not having insight into your customers' thoughts costs you exponentially more than obtaining it. When you understand how people think about your devices, you will know exactly what words they use when talking about your products and their various features. You will learn firsthand what they think your products can do, as opposed to what they can actually do. You can even ask them, for example: If you were to convince your mother/neighbor/colleague to buy this device, how would you do it? Do you think the answer to this one question would be more valuable than what you'd uncover in a survey or focus group? The very best marketing language available to you is the language of your customers.

Chapters 6 and 7 cover techniques for uncovering powerful consumer insights. Once you have them, marketing becomes much easier.

Powerful Language (Chapter 8)

Your language is the single most important component of marketing to consumers. It is the rate-determining step to the sales success of your devices. The language you use to describe your products is infinitely more important than your text-ad position on Google and your click-thru rates. It trounces page-views and Twitter engagement. But in many companies, these areas get more executive attention than the development of powerful and effective language.

Language is the key to everything. Where does it come from? How do you know what will work? That's easy: it's the same language your consumers use to describe your products. In fact, in addition to being the most important step in your marketing system, developing the right language is also the easiest. Simply understand the language your customers use and repeat it back to them. The best language is not going to come from your engineers or your marketing department. It is going to come from your customers.

You must create unquestionable perceived value before the sale. Consumers who are on their way to buy the most successful products in our business—the various Apple devices, or the Amazon Kindle, or Netflix service—are usually totally convinced that these products will be worthwhile. Usually, they're not thinking about price, even though Apple's products cost more than the competition's in almost every instance. They're not wondering whether they really need these products or services. They are convinced of their value because the companies creating these products have also created unquestionable perceived value in the market. The companies seeded the value with consumer insights and powerful language, then the consumer evangelists took over, spreading the message and pounding it home. People buying an Amazon Kindle have heard from family and friends, and they've read the endless glowing reviews on Amazon. There is no question the Kindle is terrific. (Interestingly, our industry's most successful products exceed these consumers' already very high expectations with their function, elegance, and performance.) It is not so for other products. Although people can read reviews about countless televisions, when they go to pull the trigger on one, they are usually not sure they're getting the perfect one for them. The same is true for digital cameras, computers, wireless phones, and other devices. This is a marketing shortcoming. Products with consumer evangelists, on the other hand, use a combination of powerful language and enthusiastic, loyal supporters to create a perception of certain value in the marketplace.

Industry Marketing vs. Evangelist Marketing: D-Link

➤ ➤ ➤

Industry Marketing

This information from D-Link's Web site describes their new style of wireless router.

Headline sentence

The new Xtreme N Storage Router (DIR-685) makes networking easier by combining the superior features of a wireless N router, a built-in Network Attached Storage (NAS) and a digital photo frame.

Product description

D-Link is proud to present the new Xtreme N™ Storage Router (DIR-685). By combining the superior features of a wireless N router, a built-in

CONTINUED ON FOLLOWING PAGE...

CONTINUED . . .

Network Attached Storage (NAS), digital photo frame, and D-Link Green power saving features the DIR-685 creates the ultimate user experience while conserving energy.

Experience faster speed and longer range in your home or office network with the latest 802.11n 2.4GHz wireless technology. By adding a 2.5" SATA Hard Drive, the DIR-685 allows you to share storage over your network and access files over the Internet with the built-in FTP server.

Featuring a built-in UPnP® AV server, streaming network stored videos through a compatible media player (including PlayStation® 3 and Xbox 360®) onto your television has never been easier thanks to the DIR-685.

The upright design shows off the attractive view of the 1.6 million color 3.2» LCD screen with sleek touch-sensitive buttons that provide a modern feel to allow easy control of device functions and digital display of photographs. Easily access and share your photographs from popular photo sharing sites through Frame-Channel™.

Evangelist Marketing

I will communicate what this product does for consumers, without the mind-bending technical specifications:

Our D-Link Xtreme N Storage Router not only lets you browse the Internet at home, wirelessly, at super-high speeds—but because there's a hard drive inside, you can use it to enjoy movies, photos, and music (or your documents) throughout

> the house! You can access the files on this drive from any computer (and most newer smartphones), anywhere, over the Internet. Oh, because we're revolutionizing the wireless router, there's also a 3.2-inch LCD screen here, so it's also a digital picture frame.

Mine is more technical than I would like, but I'm focusing on the outcomes, the value, rather than the high technology. This would become even more effective if I would have spoken to D-Link customers and plugged in the descriptive words they used to describe their experience with this product and routers in general.

Further, the product name, as is typical for routers, is horrendous. Did you catch how the company itself refers to its product? The D-Link *Xtreme N™ Storage Router (DIR-685)*. Wow! How about, simply, the D-Link Storage Router? And if there are bigger, better, different versions, why not call them the Storage Router 2, 3, and so on?

"To What Degree Does the Product Change Your Life?"

❖ ❖ ❖

"In our industry, we love our products and the engineers love them, and we pack features into them. But in recent years, the most successful companies have been translating the innovation they put into the product into how much it actually matters to the consumers. I think one of the other challenges is there is a pretty high bar being raised all the time—not least of which by Apple. In terms of creating evangelists: the marketing is all about to what degree does the product change your life? It starts there."

—Glenn Rogers, senior director of customer experience at Logitech

Alex's Analysis: It's fascinating to me that companies have only started talking about lifestyle in their marketing over the last couple of years, as Glenn says. And even then, I think we're seeing the best possible marketing and language from less than a handful of companies in an industry of thousands! This is not success; rather it's a willful avoidance of serving and teaching. What amazes me most is that the people who stand to benefit most are the manufacturers themselves! And yet, lifestyle-oriented marketing is treated like an unwanted burden throughout the industry.

Streamlined Public Relations (Chapter 9)

Once excellent language has been developed, it must be delivered to the media via public relations efforts and to consumers via broadcast, retail, and packaging channels. In general, as an industry, we're pretty terrible at communicating why consumers would find our products valuable. Most companies are using the wrong people to communicate with the media, and the wrong platforms to reach consumers directly.

Personal communication with media is very important. How do the largest consumer technology companies get their product information into the hands of the media? Usually, still, inexcusably, via impersonal press releases blasted to hundreds, sometimes thousands, of reporters, editors, and producers at once. The state of consumer electronics press relations is horrible. Press releases are generally embarrassing. The people distributing them can rarely answer the media's questions directly, serving only to slow down the media's progress on your story. Here's an idea: What if your executives—the ones who end up doing the interview anyway—communicated directly with the press? I realize this suggestion makes the PR industry jump, but if this were to happen at your company, it would only make your lives easier. I detail how to execute this process in Chapter 10.

Effective Platforms for Communicating Directly with Mainstream Consumers (Chapter 10)

I'll briefly examine the effectiveness of social media marketing in Chapter 10, as well as the many missed opportunities to communicate with your consumers via your product package and the (oft-missing) manuals inside.

Big Media, Not Social Media

Sorry, but mainstream consumers are not making buying decisions based on what you write on Twitter. Your "social engagement strategy" is not helping you convince today's consumers to buy your products.

There are millions of self-proclaimed social media experts on Twitter who will tell you that the very survival of your company depends on having your executives "engaging" with the Twitterati about where they're flying off to next. Please—those people are probably writing that stuff out of their parents' basements. Think about it: Have you ever made a significant investment in anything based on a Facebook advertisement? Let's take it a step further—has a Google text ad ever convinced you to buy anything right then and there? I'm not talking about search results—I mean the paid text ads. That's why there is only one valuable media when it comes to reaching mainstream consumers: big media. Television. Radio. Newspapers. Magazines. And their Web sites and blogs. Big media. And I don't just mean advertisements. I'll lay out a variety of ways to leverage big media.

Your Packaging and Manuals

What? You mean people still read manuals? Indeed. Not only that, but their experience with your manual will contribute to how they talk about your products. This doesn't get a lot of attention, but the level of frustration with product manuals is still very high among consumers. In fact, product manuals have not improved much over the last ten years. Many are written horribly, and some border on absurd comedy. I recently purchased an audio receiver for my family room entertainment center. The manual, although oversized and in many languages (the section in English was unrecognizable to me), was nearly impossible to read. A quick Google search led me to a widely respected fellow customer who wrote Web-based translations of the manual so that people could understand how to use this company's receiver! He loved the product but couldn't understand how to use it based on the manual. So he figured it out and wrote step-by-step instructions on a Web site that's now read by a high percentage of people who own this product.

Product packaging also often leaves a lot to be desired. Sometimes, it's all people have to go on to make a buying decision. (Ever ask a big-box store employee a question? What do they do? They stand next to you and read the box!) Your product's box—the package—deserves a lot more attention than you give it. It's a valuable communication platform that's neglected by most consumer electronics companies.

Facilitate and Encourage Mainstream Word-of-Mouth Communication (Chapter 11)

At this far right portion of the system, our attention shifts to the people who are the goal: mainstream consumers! So now that we've briefly touched on your product, your customer insights, your language, and your platforms, let's analyze how to approach your customers.

Encourage and nourish consumer word of mouth. All of the steps in this system are designed to create excitement—to light the flame of word-of-mouth marketing from consumer to consumer. Once you get to this rarified place, it's imperative to take steps to encourage that word of mouth. You must add kindling, oxygen, and dry wood to the fire. A critical mass of consumer word-of-mouth recommendations will push you past a tipping point for consumer evangelists.

What Evangelists Will Do for You and How to Maintain Them (Chapter 12)

Consumer evangelists will change everything. Life is different when your company enjoys consumer evangelists. There have been entire books written about what "consumer marketers" can do for you. For our purposes, though, these blessed people will tell anyone who will listen about how wonderful your product is. About how great they feel when they use it. About how they can't imagine life without your product. You aren't telling people. They are. And even though you must continue to take steps to maintain these evangelists—actually, keeping evangelists is just as challenging as creating them—your customers do a lot of the dirty work for you. I go into maintaining your consumer evangelists in Chapter 12.

Chapter Summary

Here's the process for developing consumer evangelists:

- Your product must be excellent.
- You must have deep insights about your consumers.
- You must use powerful language.
- Your public relations effort should be streamlined and improved.
- You should use powerful platforms to reach consumers directly.
- You must work to develop word-of-mouth communication among your customers.
- Once you develop evangelists, you must work to maintain them.

part two

Product Excellence

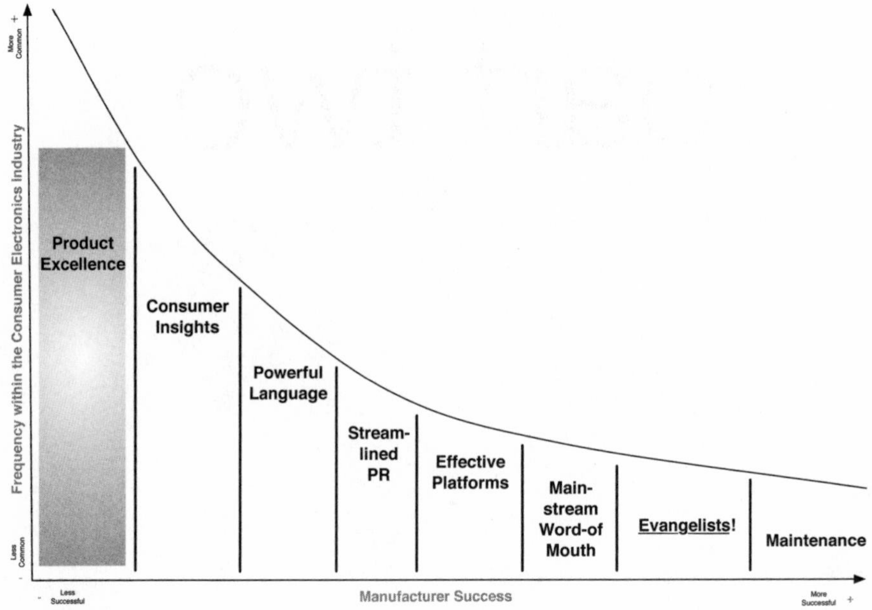
More Common +
Frequency within the Consumer Electronics Industry
Less Common -
Product Excellence
Consumer Insights
Powerful Language
Stream-lined PR
Effective Platforms
Main-stream Word-of Mouth
Evangelists!
Maintenance
- Less Successful
Manufacturer Success
More Successful +

four

Your Product: Functional Excellence

Every company selling consumer electronics today can improve sales and profit margins by marketing better, which means that their products are already very good. But the truly exceptional consumer electronics products—the ones that are perceived to be in the singular category (I laid out consumer perceptions in depth in Chapter 2)—do share some common characteristics that separate them from every other device. And it's certainly worth examining these characteristics here. At the end of this section, we'll look at which factor is more responsible for these commonalities: exceptional engineering or exceptional marketing.

To kick things off, here are the products consumers perceive to be singular. These devices are not only category defining, not only industry defining, but define our time period:

- The iPhone
- The iPad

- The Mac
- The Amazon Kindle
- Netflix

FIGURE 4.1

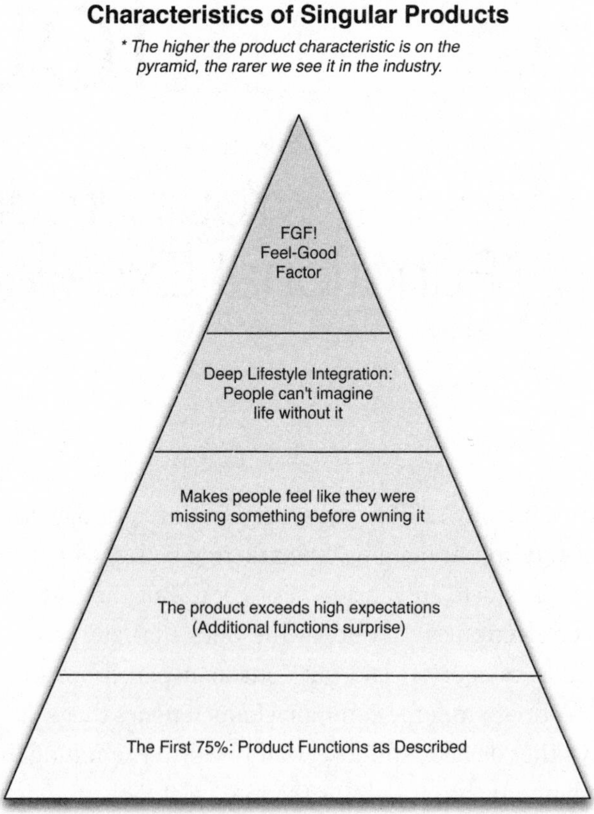
Characteristics of Singular Products
* The higher the product characteristic is on the pyramid, the rarer we see it in the industry.
FGF! Feel-Good Factor
Deep Lifestyle Integration: People can't imagine life without it
Makes people feel like they were missing something before owning it
The product exceeds high expectations (Additional functions surprise)
The First 75%: Product Functions as Described

Five products. Let's look at what they have in common.

Read this pyramid from the bottom up, as these characteristics are listed in order from most common to rarest among companies in our industry. The base of the pyramid is a prerequisite for getting onto the field of play.

Functional Excellence: The First 75 Percent

The first 75 percent of product excellence has to do with keeping your promise to consumers: the product must do what you say it does. If people buy a digital camera because you say it takes great photos, and, in fact, the photos are not sharp and rich in color and detail, you are not keeping your promise to consumers. If people buy a Bluetooth mouse for their computer, but the mouse is impossible to discover and pair with the PC, you are breaking your promise. If your software doesn't do what you say it does, if your hardware is missing features that you promise, if your service does not deliver what you described, you are not delivering on your promises. People must feel like they are getting what was expected. Most products at retail today execute this perfectly well. You don't really have a choice. There are systems in place to make sure the first 75 percent of product excellence exists in your devices. If your product didn't deliver on your promise:

- The retail buyers—whether at Best Buy, Amazon, or elsewhere—would prevent it from reaching the shelves.
- The critics in the press and on tech blogs would hammer the device.
- Consumers would do so as well in online reviews.

Guy Kawasaki on Marketing Consumer Electronics

The following is an email conversation with Guy Kawasaki, founder of Alltop.com and former chief evangelist at Apple.

On what keeps most consumer electronics manufacturers from attaining consumer evangelists:

CONTINUED ON FOLLOWING PAGE…

CONTINUED . . .

There is one primary reason: Their products [stink]. It's very hard to get evangelists for a [stinky] product. You have to have a great product [to attain evangelists].

On why technology makers are still so inexcusably terrible at communicating with consumers:

> This befuddles me too. They must never use their own products, so they don't know how to explain them to customers. At the very least, they should practice on their spouses and parents. If they can't understand what you make, no one can.

On the most damaging marketing problem in consumer electronics today:

> The user interface of products. This goes back to the previous question. When your spouse or parents can use your product by themselves, you're on the way. When they can use it without a manual, you've arrived.

Alex's Analysis: There has been great improvement in the quality of consumer electronics, and I disagree with Guy on his first point: most of the products on the mainstream market today are perfectly acceptable. They may not be truly great, but the vast majority do what they promise. And that's the 75 percent of the product excellence battle. The remaining 25 percent required to achieve singular product status, which I lay out in the rest of this chapter, is much rarer.

I couldn't agree more with Guy's other point about engineers not using their own products. More specifically, I actually believe that your engineers aren't capable of thinking about your products from the perspective of your consumers. These engineers are so technical, and their thinking is so ingrained and rooted in technical processes and specifications that they cannot put themselves into a mainstream consumer's shoes.

This first 75 percent is simply a prerequisite for playing the game of consumer electronics. It's assumed. That's why I often say that the vast majority of consumer electronics on today's market are quite good, simply because they deliver on what was promised. You have no choice. Conversely, you are not very good at the final 25 percent of product excellence.

Let's review these more elusive product qualities that singular products have in spades.

Singular Products Exceed Expectations

By the time people decide to purchase one of the five singular products, they've heard the buzz and processed the hype. Everyone is talking about them, right? People have seen the products around: their friends have these devices. They've seen the Kindle on the train. Their family members enjoy and talk about Netflix. And who hasn't talked to Mac lovers who endlessly prod their Windows-using counterparts about when they're going to switch over? (Seriously, how are there so many of these people? Depending on which study you read, Mac's market share is right around 5 percent worldwide, although Windows owns over 90 percent of the market. I guess it's a testament to Apple's wildly powerful marketing that 5 percent of the users are making 90 percent of the noise. Did you ever hear a Windows person cajoling a Mac person to switch to Microsoft? Me neither.) The point is that people are familiar with singular products. Do note, however, that the manufacturer is responsible for very little of what the consumers are seeing and hearing. Other consumers are doing the one-to-one marketing. This is what life is like for companies who have consumer evangelists. There has been buildup. Expectations are in place, and they're rather high.

And yet, when people finally acquire these technologies, they are usually more impressed than they ever expected. The product so exceeds their expectations that they start talking about it to their own friends and families. They literally can't contain themselves. For example, when I got my iPad, I expected that I would like it. But I was shocked at just how much I liked it. I did not expect it to become a part of my daily workflow so quickly and easily. It replaced the vast majority of my need for my computer, in a small, convenient, feel-good, sexy package (more on the elusive Feel Good Factor later in this chapter). My wife said the same thing after she got her Amazon Kindle e-book reader. She was blown away by how much she enjoyed reading on it; it was comfortable, incredibly easy, and the Kindle actually sped up the already fast rate at which my wife devours books.

Surprising Additional Functionality

Netflix is a great example of how a product exceeds expectations by surprising customers with excellent, unforeseen additional functionality. Take the streaming options: they're constantly growing. We learned in 2011 that Netflix spent tens of millions of dollars to land the exclusive rights to a television show starring Kevin Spacey. So subscribers will get twenty-six episodes that others will not see. This was not only a surprise, but almost a reward for being a customer. When Netflix pricing model changed in mid-2011, increasing the cost of the service for many customers, a lot of them justified the added expense with all of the new content they're getting. Netflix also surprises users with the accuracy of its recommendations. Based on your ratings for movies and shows, Netflix suggests other works you would likely enjoy. Some people like this feature so much they start rating everything they've ever seen, just to take better advantage of the suggestions. People thought they were signing up for one or two DVDs per month, only to discover these huge additional benefits at absolutely no extra cost.

Let's look at the Amazon Kindle. Customers expect to buy books and read them. But one wildly useful feature that is constantly talked about by consumers is the ability to preview books for free immediately. It's one thing to read customer reviews. It's entirely another experience to read sample pages from a book to see if it's right for you. Of course, the very same capability has existed on Amazon's Web site for years. But the fact it's available on the Kindle—which is considered a warm-and-fuzzy reader by most of its users, the opposite of their feelings for their PC—happily surprises people and only solidifies their love for the product.

The iPad and the iPhone are basically small computers, and so their applications are endless. But people acquire them with certain visions of how they'll be used. For example, I suspected I'd enjoy looking at photos and movies of my children on the iPad. I wasn't sure if I'd like browsing the Internet on it (I love the experience), but I figured it wouldn't be primarily used for that. What I didn't suspect was that it would become so central in my personal organization and productivity. It has replaced my computer—and, in a great surprise to me, even paper—for my project and task management. I'm a big pen and paper guy. I like how they feel. I like the process of writing with a real pen. But you know what? I like writing on the iPad more. Talk to ten people about what surprises them most about their iPad or their iPhone, and each one will tell you something different. For example, I've heard people say they never thought they'd be downloading any apps at all but are now browsing the app store every single day. I've also heard people say that they love staying on top of their social media on their iPhone far more than with their computer. Others are amazed that they can use a cloud file storage tool like Dropbox and access their important documents from anywhere, using any device, from multiple computers to their smartphone to their tablet.

Value Expansion

Another area where singular products excel is expansion. The most successful products in consumer electronics improve during the time that consumers own them. This expansion is built into the user experience, and it's another way that these products exceed consumers' expectations.

Netflix expands its offerings on what feels like a monthly basis. There are constant deals with cable networks, movie houses, and new content arrivals. People have significantly more viewing options on Netflix today than they did six months ago. Not only that, but the company keeps adding devices to its arsenal of consumption options. Once upon a time, all you got from Netflix were DVDs. Then it expanded into streaming on your computer. Then Netflix started streaming to video game consoles, then some Internet-connected DVD players, then onto the TiVo® DVR, then it was on the iPhone and the iPad and all those Android phones. In my home alone, I can watch Netflix on eleven different devices, counting computers, phones, tablets, TiVo, and video game consoles. When I'm on the road, far from home, all three mobile devices I carry—laptop, iPhone, and iPad—get Netflix. It didn't used to be this way, but Netflix expanded, far surpassing most people's expectations of what they were going to get for about $8 to $16 per month.

Of course, the iPhone and iPad (and, although they are not singular products, all the Android devices) are endlessly expandable thanks to the hundreds of thousands of downloadable apps that are available. There was once a time when we bought a wireless phone and it was a closed system. Remember that? We used it as it came out of the box for years. Over the years, phones like the Palm Treo—the first proper smartphone—Blackberry devices, and Nokia phones "opened" themselves to external applications. But it was so complicated. You had to go to the developer's Web site, probably on your computer, download the app, and then synchronize it over to the phone through a USB cable. And if all that worked, you had one new app. What Apple pioneered and perfected was an easy way to do this quickly and for multiple apps. The app store is always available, with hundreds of thousands of options to make your phone better. Want to play a game? Want to listen to music? Want to edit your pictures? It's endless, built-in expansion. It's brilliant. For consumers, today's app stores morph the phone—and the tablet—into a device of endless possibilities. What do I want the phone to become tomorrow? It's up to me.

Talk about surpassing expectations.

Further, Apple and Google release periodic operating system upgrades that improve the device experience significantly. These are downloadable updates that increase the functionality of their products. One of Apple's most acclaimed updates was the release of iOS 4, which brought multitasking and something as simple as folders to the home screens of people's phones. Customers found it hugely valuable.

Amazon's Kindle is expandable in similar ways. You can load it with whatever books you like. You can subscribe to newspapers. You can read PDF documents on it. But Amazon was brilliant to create Kindle reading opportunities on non-Kindle devices. One of my wife's favorite Kindle features is the ability to read a few pages of her current book on her iPhone when she has a couple of extra minutes. Her books are always with her. And the mind-blowing part is that it keeps her place across all the devices: when she returns to the Kindle, the book is ready to go, right where she stopped reading on her phone.

The key to all of this is that not only do these singular devices improve dramatically over the span of consumer ownership, but they do so at no cost. People get more constantly without paying an extra penny (unless they choose to, in the case of the app store, but there is plenty of value there for free).

Holy Cow Moments

The exceeding of expectations and the built-in expansion of value combine to lead to an invaluable collective expression of wonderment among consumers. I call them *Holy Cow Moments*. It's a communication of the ways these products have blown consumers away. It makes people who do not yet own the products say "Wow." It makes non-owners imagine themselves using your products. It goes a long way toward creating powerful word-of-mouth buzz among consumers (which I cover in depth in Chapter 11). The end result is priceless to manufacturers.

Because it is very difficult to communicate that your product exceeds people's expectations, and because consumer electronics makers have a difficult time with basic, easy marketing tasks (like sending out a well-written, compelling press release), manufacturers—even these, the very best marketers in the business—do not draw attention to how their products surprise their customers. As such, these companies are indirectly perceived by consumers as underselling their value. It's not that these manufacturers don't talk about these extra features—they do, and more importantly, consumers do—but consumers are not prepared for the very high value they receive from these surprising additional features. All of which, added together, shine a glowing light on the manufacturers within their target market. This is what happens when you so dramatically exceed your customers' expectations.

Perceived Quality of Life

Another phenomenon that occurs with the most exceptional products is that excited, surprised, and overjoyed consumers begin to take stock of their lives with the product as compared to life without it. It usually takes three to six months of product ownership for consumers to get to this point. This is because people must have an opportunity to use the product intensively over an extended period of time. The product's tentacles must be given time to wrap themselves around the various aspects of its consumers' lives. Once they get to this product–life integration point, where the huge value of the device is easy to identify—and consumers have had plenty of practice singing the products' praises, both verbally and in their thoughts—people start to assess the bigger impact. They look back, remembering life before product ownership, and they look forward, imagining what life would be like if they lost the great things this device does for them: *I was missing so much before I had this.* And, even more valuable to manufacturers: *I can't imagine my life without this product.* If your customers think this, you will rule the world.

Here's what that thought process looks like:

FIGURE 4.2

Perceived Quality of Life

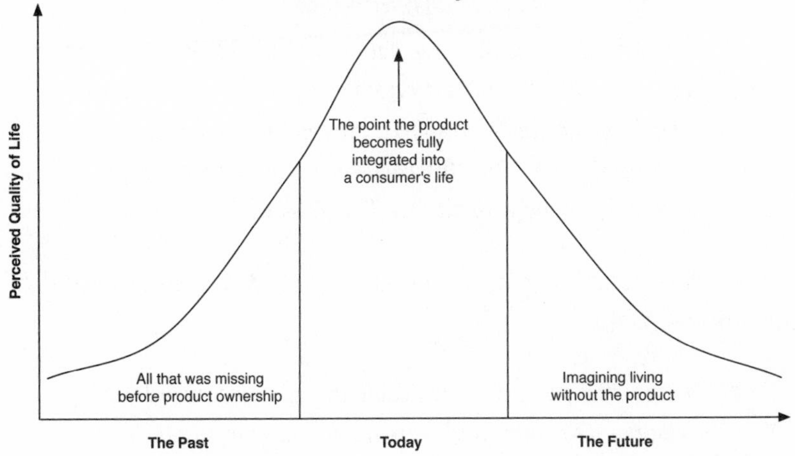

This bell curve is the consumer's perceived quality of life as it relates to singular products. The middle of the curve is the present, which is the point at which the product has become fully integrated into the consumer's life. The area to the left of the curve is the less attractive past, which involves the consumer wondering how he or she lived without all that this device offers. And the right of the curve involves imagining the future: *How could I live without this?*

Let's look at both perceptions.

Makes People Realize What They Were Missing

After people find their expectations exceeded by exceptional products, and after they take stock of the features that surprise them, they begin to think about what life was like before they owned this product. After having an opportunity to integrate the product into their lives, people begin to realize all that they were missing. For example:

- *The picture on this HDTV is so amazing. How did I live without it?*
- *I can't believe how organized this iPad keeps me. How did I get by with just pen and paper before?*
- *Not only can I have conversations on my iPhone, but I can check in with friends on Facebook, tweet, read my books, watch movies and TV shows, play games, look up recipes, and access the entire Internet—from my phone! Seriously, how did I get by without this iPhone—ever?!*

The less desirable version of this—if your product does not thrill consumers—is this:

- *I sure miss my TiVo. This cable digital video recorder costs less, but it's clunky, and there are no recommendations. And it has even missed taping shows late at night.*
- *I like this Canon digital SLR just fine, but all my old lenses are for my Nikon. And there was something comfortable about that old Nikon.*
- *This shopping site has a lot of products, but I don't get free two-day shipping like I do on my usual shopping site. And I miss all the reviews my usual site has.*

People Can't Imagine Living Without the Product

People who are particularly passionate about their new technology also cannot imagine living without the product. The functionalities they have come to love have such a positive impact on them that they can't stand to bear the thought of losing them: *Now that I've had the iPhone/Android phone, I could never use another phone. Sure, it's expensive to pay for all the minutes, and all the data, but it's so worth it.* People start to imagine the conveniences they would have to give up if they no longer used this device, and it's not a reality they are willing to live in.

The other side of this, for products that don't excite consumers—for many of the products on the market today—is that people simply never get to this point. They are not particularly moved by products that they perceive as commodities. They don't see their life as being particularly improved. Even if it actually is, they have less awareness of it. They never really think about living without the product because it is almost like they are living without it already. The worst-case scenario for particularly terrible products (and there aren't many of these) is that people envision a better future without your product. This really only happens with devices that are technically broken and need to be returned or exchanged or ones that don't even get to the base of our product excellence pyramid. They don't keep their promise to consumers. They don't do what the manufacturer says they do.

The FGF: Feel Good Factor

The most popular consumer electronics, and particularly the ones in the singular category, all elicit a very important feeling of satisfaction for customers. It's the same sort of warm-and-fuzzy feelings that children often create, and I am not blowing this out of proportion. Parents feel responsible for their children's achievements and successes. Consumers feel a similar sense of pride when they make the right buying decision for a product they perceive as exceptional. I call this phenomenon the *feel good factor* or FGF.

Here's what FGF sounds like—I'm sure you've heard it from some of your friends or family. Maybe you've even experienced it.

- *I am amazed by this phone.*
- *The picture on the TV is amazing. I've never seen anything like it. I'll never watch anything that's not in high definition anymore.*
- *I record the video and the grandparents can see the footage in seconds. It's unbelievable.*
- *I can't believe how much I love this. I thought I'd like it well enough, but I'm blown away.*

People often feel this way about their vehicles, particularly luxury cars, or fine restaurants. But in those cases, it is to be expected because automobiles and fine dining establishments are all about experience and emotion. You spend countless hours in a car, and there is a prestige that comes with high-end vehicles. And fine dining is often done around special events and creates long-term memories. But technology is generally perceived as cold and difficult by the mainstream, which is why it's a wonder that certain products and services can attain this highest level of consumer success.

So, let's break it down. These singular products share some features, and create strong emotions for their consumers.

- ***Physically, it feels good to hold the product.***
  Although the iPhone is about the same shape as a number of phones from many different manufacturers—including Nokia, Research in Motion, and LG—there is something that separates its physical form factor from the competition: slickness, smoothness, richness, elegance. Of course, Apple pays more attention to the physical look and feel of its products than any other manufacturer, so this is not a surprise. It's also not a surprise that so many Android phones have assumed the same general shape as the iPhone—big screen, touchscreen, and less than a handful of buttons. It's also no accident that Amazon's Kindle is a pleasure to hold in one's hands: light, smooth, and almost silky plastic. It's clear that the Kindle's designers worked hard to create a product that's physically elegant. In the case of Netflix, where there is no product to speak of, the physical "feel good" is in the interface; whether you're using Netflix on your computer, your phone, or via your video game system, the interface is intuitive, easy, elegant, and wildly useful. Have you noticed? Elegance is very important. Of course, there are countless other products that feel good in the hands, but this is one characteristic that all of the singular products have in common.

As a preview to the next section, this "physical" portion of the FGF is executed by your engineers. But make no mistake: the engineers at this company are guided (which is a sweet way of saying pushed, cajoled, and prodded) by executives who understand that excellent product physicality is the first step in creating FGF, and, ultimately, singular products that enjoy consumer evangelists. Then, marketing should take over to make sure that consumers learn about, and evangelize, these devices.

- ***The first impression is stunning.***

What's the first impression? Why, the packaging of course. Nine out of ten companies in our industry take packaging for granted. When you buy a mobile device from Apple, the packaging is just as "feel good" as the product. Ever see a Kindle box? It's simple, slick, and inviting, just like the Kindle. This is no accident. Your packaging is your first impression for consumers. If your functionally excellent device comes in a boring white box, then you are not taking advantage of one of the easiest and most important marketing opportunities available to you. Your packaging should be a sneak preview of the good feelings that await your customers once they start using your device. Netflix does it every time you get a DVD in the mail. Every time you see that red envelope in the mailbox, you know there's entertainment waiting for you—a night with your significant other or your kids on the couch, with drinks, food, and the comfort of home. That's what Netflix has trained its millions of customers to feel when they see that red envelope.

I've had really smart executives of some very successful companies ask me this question: *Isn't packaging less important now that people are buying so many of our products online?* I tell them they're thinking about it all wrong.

Sure, the packaging might influence consumers in making a buying decision, but even at bricks-and-mortar retail, a lot of packaging isn't even visible anymore. It's mostly locked away. On the contrary, your packaging should be designed to build anticipation between the purchase and the start of use. Use it to train people how to think about your products. Even if that moment is less than one minute—the time between opening up the outer mail order box and opening your package—you are missing an opportunity to excite your customers. If your packaging can get someone to think, *Wow, that's innovative*, or, *That's brilliant!* they're in the right frame of mind to begin a long, wonderful relationship with your product and your company. Shift your mindset, and use your packaging as a proper introduction to your devices for new customers.

- ***Singular products are fashionable.***

  A big part of the FGF that singular products create is that people feel like they're getting something fashionable when they buy them, and, just as importantly, use them. There's something supremely modern about pulling out the latest and greatest device that's in the news. People want to be seen with it. For some people, the singular product actually becomes a fashion accessory. People want to be asked about it, and they're happy to tell anyone who asks about their experiences. It feels good to be noticed. Attention feels good. Gucci is boring. Prada may be difficult for many people even to identify. But everyone knows an iPhone. And people wonder what it's like to read books on that Kindle. They've seen it on the news. It's new. It's cool. It's fashionable.

  Then there's this: when people buy an iPhone or a Kindle or a Mac, there is a sense of community that comes in that box. Do not underestimate the power of the perception of belonging to a community that's hip, happy, satisfied, and fashionable. Although they'll never say it publicly, Apple is well aware of the strong sense of affiliation its customers feel with each other. This is particularly evident when you see one of those middle-of-the-night lines the day Apple launches a new product. Those Apple fanatics who camp out overnight and spend eight or twelve or twenty-four hours waiting together, giddy with an excitement that I can only compare to waiting for tickets to a concert or playoff sporting event. *Our team is going to go to the Super Bowl! We're going to get the new iPhone!* These folks are in it together, they're out there, cold, sleepless, and unbelievably excited—sitting in lawn chairs or right on the cold cement of the sidewalk.

People who aren't a part of that core community of inner circle evangelists—they see what's going on. Remember, the lines are on the nightly news on every station in the country. There are photos of these people, anticipation on their faces, in newspapers the next morning. This is not happening in a bubble. And when mainstream consumers see this, the seeds of wonder are planted. And for some consumers, these seeds take root, they germinate, and finally grow into a sense of desire. For the product but also for the community. People desire to attain that joy. And why not? If spending $300 or $400 on a gadget makes these hip, interesting people happy, then maybe I need that gadget, too. Maybe it'll make me happy, too.

- ***Singular products are aspirations attained.***

To return to our previous analogy, it's easy to see how singular technology shares another characteristic with luxury cars and the finest dining establishments. People aspire to drive the finest vehicles. They crave the feeling

> of an expensive car, especially if they've been thinking and dreaming about it for a while. You're probably familiar with the feeling: you start to notice the car on the road more. Suddenly, you know exactly where the dealerships are. You check Web sites again and again. You're just window-shopping at first, but then the craving grows.
>
> Fine dining establishments are even more similar to consumer electronics. You've heard about them from friends or family or maybe in the news. You start to read reviews—both from the experts and then fellow diners. You look at the menu online. You wonder what it would be like to eat there. It sounds so delicious, so you start checking the review sites more regularly, looking for more recent experiences. Dining at this restaurant becomes a goal. It's a destination. You aspire to eat there.

The very best consumer electronics are no different.

People aspire to own an iPhone or a Kindle or a Mac or an iPad. It's true that some people can make an impulse decision and pull the trigger on one of these products without much thought or planning. But most consumers put a lot of thought into buying a smartphone or a computer or an e-book reader or a tablet. Sure, they're expensive, and that's as a good a reason as any to analyze a buying decision carefully.

But these are also very personal products. A smartphone connects you to your family when you are away from it. When I am on the road, my smartphone is the tool that keeps me in touch with my wife and children. When I am half a world away, my smartphone literally brings me the comfort of home. I damn well better select the right smartphone to do this most important of jobs. Similarly, people will spend countless hours with their desktop and laptop computers. And a Kindle is a gadget that takes the place of thousands of books—meaning tens of thousands of hours, and in personal places at that—in bed, on the couch, on vacation, and on the beach. So, rightfully, these intensely personal product purchases are carefully planned.

And in that planning, an aspiration gradually develops. People have ample opportunity to observe happy owners of the devices they're thinking about: people they know, people they see on the news, and people they hear about (*My sister just* loves *her Kindle*). Much as they do with restaurants, people begin active research, as opposed to the passive data collection that occurs when they hear about these devices.

- People hit the Internet and start to collect professional reviews. Their interest grows.
- They head to consumer review sites, and start reading about the experiences of their peers. Interest turns into desire.
- They head to the blogs (maybe), and go through an "unboxing" article, which is a half-step short of actually opening the box themselves. Desire develops into aspiration.
- They start to imagine themselves using or owning the device.
- They begin to have dreams about it. (From personal experience, I know that this really happens! You probably do, too.)

This aspiration phenomenon occurs most intensely with singular products. Most mainstream consumers don't dream about a Windows-based desktop computer. Similarly, they don't imagine themselves watching a Samsung HDTV, any more than they imagine themselves watching an LG or Sony or Vizio TV. They might very well dream about an HDTV on their wall, just as they may dream about owning a digital camera, but those dreams are manufacturer agnostic. The makers of those technologies are interchangeable in consumers' wishes.

That's the magic of what the manufacturers of singular products have accomplished—people aspire to own their products specifically. They need an Apple device or a Kindle instead of their competitors' devices. People want to join "the club" of these companies' products, even if it's only a club they've created in their minds. It's a deadly competitive advantage.

Singular products are comforting.

In the previous section, I detailed how singular products are personal in nature. Across the board, they are also generally perceived as comforting. As I've already described, the iPhone keeps consumers connected to their loved ones when they cannot be with them physically. You "curl up" with a Kindle, and you escape into the stories it brings you. Or you learn from nonfiction that can change your life for the better. On a gadget! The Mac and the iPad are similarly personal. You spend countless hours on these devices, and they bring you information you seek or allow you to engage in productive work that's critical to your success. How is Netflix personal? Wherever you are, at home, on vacation, or on business travel in a lonely hotel, the $7.99 per month Netflix service brings you movies and television shows that connect you with your favorite characters or bring you joy and entertainment. Whether on the big-screen TV in your family room, on the smartphone screen on the airplane, or on a laptop or tablet device while away from home, Netflix lets you watch what you want, and as much of it as you want. That's comforting.

Products that are not perceived as singular can also sometimes be perceived as comforting—but only from a product category standpoint rather than from a brand perspective. My digital camera captures special moments in my children's lives. It captures the memories of my own life. But people rarely think that their Kodak is capturing the memories of their lives. They rarely process that their Canon HD digital camcorder is capturing the home movies of their lives. They simply think, *My digital camcorder is capturing my home movies, and that's great.* The difference is that the singular products make people think that the brand is comforting to them, and commodities allow people to think that the style of product is comforting. It's a hellacious difference. It's the distance between being hugely successful and simply average.

Executives, Engineers, and Marketers (Oh My!)

Three key groups within your organization are involved in breathing life into singular products:

- High-level executives with a specific vision of the kind of customer experiences they want to create,
- Talented engineers who can create excellent products, and
- Terrific marketing leaders, who frame the product in a way that captures the public's ongoing interest.

Here is what this interaction looks like:

FIGURE 4.3

The Three Groups Involved in Creating Singular Products

And what happens when only two of the three are involved

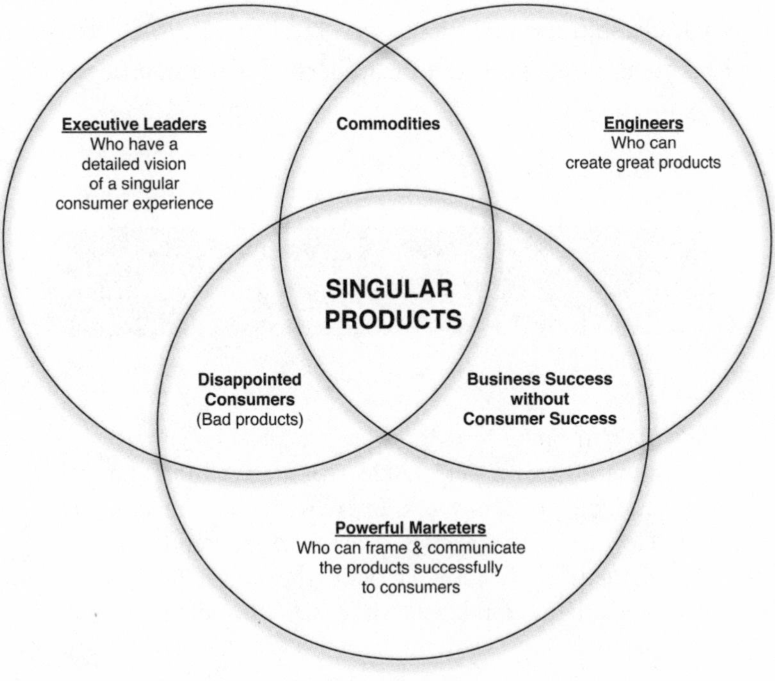

The Executive Leaders

The most successful companies in consumer electronics have chief executives who have a crystal-clear vision of the kind of customer experience they want to create and the product that can do this. Apple's CEO, Steve Jobs, is known to micromanage even the smallest product details until they are to his liking. He insists that the user experience be singular. He admits to keeping Apple focused sharply on a handful of products and making them excellent—to the exclusion of hundreds of other product possibilities, even if they can be good sources of revenue for Apple. Just because you can do something doesn't mean that you should. Jeff Bezos, Amazon's CEO, is also known for clearly articulating his vision for the Amazon Kindle and then challenging his engineers to execute it.

Neither the iPhone nor the Kindle would be as wildly popular with the public as they are without the exacting visions of their respective companies' chief executives. These CEOs also have an executive team around them that is tightly in tune with what the CEO is looking for. In order to attain their ideal customer experience, the company's highest leadership specifies the smallest product details. Of course, this can backfire in three seconds if the leadership is not in tune with what

"He Makes the Decisions About These Products"

"When Steve Jobs introduces a product, it's always about his personal love of the product. The audience is dying to know what he has created. He makes the decisions about these products. Remember, he doesn't build them, but he designs them. You have to have CEO leadership

> that can go from design of product or service to design of the communication."
>
> —John Sculley, former CEO of Apple
>
> ***Alex's Analysis:*** In early 2011, the *New York Times* published an article that lauded Steve Jobs as Apple's "tastemaker." His decisions about which product to develop and how to design it are based on instinct of what consumers will be passionate about. Since his return as Apple CEO in 1997, Jobs has overseen the wild successes of the iMac, iPod, iPhone, and the iPad, not to mention the back-end systems that some argue are more purely responsible for Apple's success than any hardware, like the iTunes Music Store and the App Store. The chief executive's instincts for consumers must be honed and refined.

consumers want. That's critical here; otherwise, your executives are micromanaging the creation of mediocre products.

The Engineers

Engineering is most responsible for creating excellent products. They execute on their executives' vision, when there is one, and bring their own ideas into product development. They make the product easy to use (although some would argue they actually make a product difficult to use). They make the product intuitive. They create, develop, and build functionality. Engineering's good work here is a prerequisite for mainstream retail distribution.

The Marketers

This is often the missing link in consumer electronics, and it's the whole reason I'm writing this book. For companies creating singular products, their marketers are talented enough to alert, motivate, and excite the masses about their products. The most successful products in our business are long-lived, so marketers at these companies face the unique challenge of keeping consumers excited about a product line for years (think iPod and iPhone).

Singular products are only developed when all three types of people are functioning at a high level and communicating effectively. Singular products can only be created at the intersection of executives with a specific vision of user experience, engineers who can execute on that vision, and marketers who can communicate the magic that has been created. These factors must all come together before a legendary device can come to life in our business.

If only two of the three are working together, like when there are executives with vision and engineers who can execute on that vision but poor marketing initiative, you have a recipe for pumping commodities into the market. This is the scenario for many companies in our industry, and likely what you see at your own company or your clients' companies. Of the three components, good marketing is missing most often. Commodities are good or excellent products that suffer from a lack of effective marketing. They are good enough to make it to the mainstream retail market but not good enough to rise above the fray of all the other commodities with which they are competing. So, inexcusably, these products are left to languish in perceived mediocrity. Perhaps their product name is terrible. Perhaps they are priced inappropriately (yes, pricing is marketing). Maybe you are using the wrong language to describe these products. Or maybe you're not reaching people via the best possible platforms. Missing any one of these steps can suck a product from potential singular or at least special status right down into commodity status.

When there are executives with vision and good marketers but poor engineers, it leads to a quick burst of good sales of a bad product. This scenario is not often seen in our business. This quickly creates disappointed, sometimes angry, consumers who put a quick stop to good sales. We don't see this phenomenon in our industry because it's a self-policing environment. As I've mentioned previously, usually retail buyers will put the kibosh on poor products. Or media reviewers will. Or bloggers, who review early units, will describe just how bad the product is. But sometimes a product falls through the cracks and momentarily goes mainstream, angering the masses.

When there are good marketers and good engineers but leadership without a specific product vision, you usually end up with sales success but little "consumer success," meaning people will use your products because you effectively communicated their value to the market, but the user experience is rarely special (because that typically comes from exacting executives). So people don't get as excited about these products. They don't talk about them as much. Their timeline for real sales success is much shorter than singular products, which have all three elements. These devices rarely exceed consumers' expectations. And they rarely create Holy Cow moments. They are good, effective products that never generate significant consumer energy.

Chapter Summary

Functional excellence is assumed and required to make it to market in consumer electronics. Singular products, which are the most successful consumer technologies, share these characteristics:

- They exceed consumers' already high expectations.
- They have unexpected additional functionalities.
- Their functionality, and therefore their value, actually expands over the time that consumers own them, usually at no cost.
- These devices generate Holy Cow moments for consumers.
- When consumers fully integrate a singular product into their lives, they realize what they were missing before owning it.

- Consumers can't imagine life without this device or service.

Singular products have a high feel good factor (FGF). FGF is made up of these characteristics:

- The product feels good physically.
- It makes a terrific first impression.
- The technology is fashionable.
- The product is an aspiration attained.
- The device is comforting to consumers.

The creation of singular products requires the successful interaction of three groups inside your company:

- Top executives with a specific vision of the customer experience they want to create,
- Excellent engineers who can executive on this vision, and
- Marketers who can reach and energize consumers about your devices.

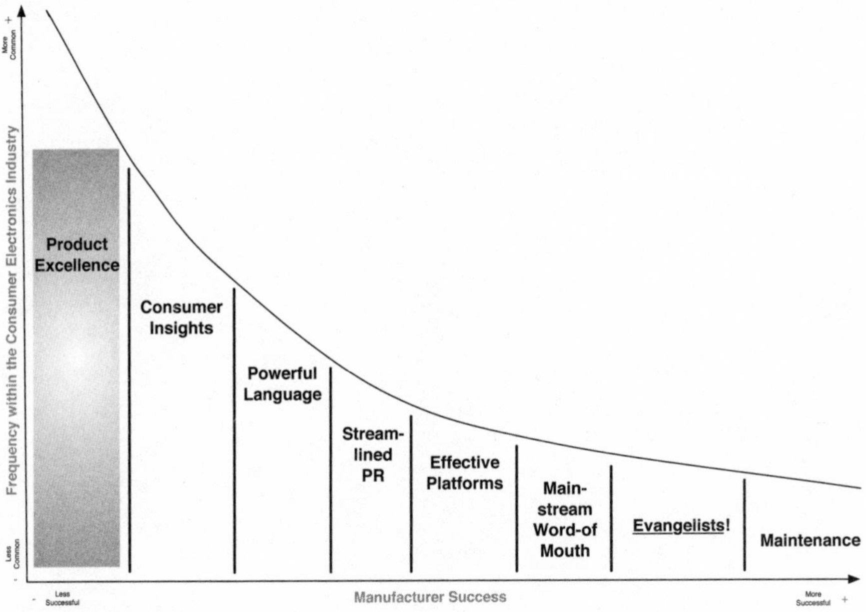

Frequency within the Consumer Electronics Industry
More Common +
- Less Common
Product Excellence
Consumer Insights
Powerful Language
Stream-lined PR
Effective Platforms
Main-stream Word-of Mouth
Evangelists!
Maintenance
Manufacturer Success
- Less Successful
More Successful +

five

Product Names and Prices

This chapter moves beyond product functionality to two key marketing tools at your disposal: the names you give your devices and the prices you assign them. These two details must fall strictly under the function of your marketing department. These are marketing decisions, not engineering ones. Nobody but your marketing team should be determining these critical details. The name of your product will contribute little to its success, but it will have much to do with its failure. Similarly, pricing your devices appropriately does not automatically create success. But the wrong price point guarantees failure with consumers.

These are crucial details, not just for the success of the specific products or services, but for the overall success of your company. The irony is that product names and pricing are easy to get right, but most companies screw up naming their product, and many manufacturers price their devices outside of consumers' expectations. This chapter will describe how to establish effective product names and appropriate pricing.

Terrible Product Names

This is so important and so easy to get right that the point must be driven home. This is one of those "if you only come away with one thing" points, so please read closely. Consumer electronics product names, almost across the board, are horrible, embarrassing, unnecessarily technical, far too long, and completely unhelpful to consumers—or manufacturers. Products in our industry are named as if their makers really don't want consumers ever to be able to remember or repeat the name of their device. They spend millions of dollars researching, engineering, and marketing these products, sometimes tens of millions, and sometimes hundreds of millions. And yet, the vast majority of companies screw up something as easy and as important as the name of these products.

If, at the time of this writing, you were shopping for a Windows-based laptop, you could have chosen between the Toshiba Satellite L645D-S4036 LED TruBrite 14-Inch Laptop (Black), the HP Pavilion dv6-3013nr 15.6-Inch Laptop Argento, the Dell Inspiron i14R-1708MRB 14-Inch Laptop (Mars Black), or the Acer AS5742-7653 15.6-Inch Laptop (Mesh Black). These names are copied right from Amazon's Web site. Maybe laptops require complicated names.

So let's look at high-definition televisions. If you like Panasonic, you can choose the Panasonic TC-L32U22 32-Inch 1080p LCD HDTV. Want an LG? Maybe you should go for the LG 37LE5300 37-Inch 1080p 120 Hz LED LCD HDTV. Vizio has become a popular seller over the last couple of years. You can purchase their VIZIO M260MV 26-Inch 1080p LED LCD HDTV with Razor LED Backlighting, Black. Or, if you're a fan of Samsung, you can pull the trigger on a Samsung LN55C650 55-Inch 1080p 120 Hz LCD HDTV (Black). You'll find these shockingly ineffective product names and model numbers across the entire spectrum of the industry.

Jared Newman, a writer for the technology blog *Technologizer*, asked Samsung to help decipher its television product names. The company complied, and here is what the Samsung UN55C7000 means to the people who named it:

- UN means that the screen technology is LED, a kind of LCD display.
- 55 is the screen size—this TV is 55 inches.
- The letter C signifies that this television was made in 2010. In 2011, this letter changed to D, and so on.
- Finally, 7000 is the series number, which, it turns out, reflects that this television is of an ultra-slim design, has a resolution of 1080p, and enjoys a 240Hz refresh rate.

So there you go. The only thing that makes sense in these details is the 55. Everything else might as well be in a foreign language. These codes only have significance to the people who made them up. I would confidently bet my children's college money that most of the people who work at Samsung don't know that UN somehow translates to LED. And the thing is, all of the companies whose product names I've listed above have the same kind of crib-sheet definitions for the various components of their model numbers. It's fine to use these product numbers to identify these devices internally, inside the four walls of your company. The problem is that these companies are using their model numbers to reference their products publicly, and expecting consumers to understand what they mean. I'll have more on this public vs. private identification soon.

"Acronyms Are Only Relevant to the Industry"

"The industry competes with itself with language and acronyms that are only relevant to the industry. They are not relevant to the consumer. They try to one up each other on a technological benefit that doesn't mean anything. We were

CONTINUED ON FOLLOWING PAGE...

CONTINUED . . .

really the first brand in the U.S. to say we are not going to call the phone by its technological name. We gave every handset a name, not a tech code."

—Bob Stoherer, vice president of marketing, Virgin Mobile

Alex's Analysis: Why do you do this? Why are these products given names that are interesting and meaningful to you but not consumers? Probably 90 percent of consumer electronics companies name their products this way. The irony is that most of your own staff does not know what the codes in these product names signify. You're not just confusing your intended market—you're confusing your own company.

How Terrible Product Names Kill Good Products

What's wrong with this picture? What isn't wrong might be a better question. Here are nine problems with these undecipherable, never-ending, self-serving product names:

1. Product names are far too long. There is no reason to impose ten-word product names with eight-character model numbers on consumers.
2. They are far too complicated. See problem number 1.
3. Your product names are impossible to remember. Let's say somebody is interested in learning more about your device. This would be impossible unless they write down (or copy and paste) the name of the device. You are pre-emptively preventing consumers from remembering the

name of your technology, and also from talking about it to their friends, family, and colleagues.

4. They don't allow consumers to reference your device or your company in their thoughts or in conversation with other people. When you name your product with complicated combinations of letters and numbers, you are killing any chance at word-of-mouth buzz among consumers.
5. The media is also locked out by these product names. With today's tiny attention spans, if you can't name and identify your device to editors, reporters, and producers quickly and easily, you're out of luck. LN55P60X-II will get your pitch deleted every time.
6. Conversely, the only people these product names help are the few internal employees who understand what each part of the product name refers to. The industry's wildly complicated names are outwardly meaningless but clearly serve a purpose for a few people internally. They help engineers, and maybe customer service reps, to differentiate between products. You may know exactly what each device is immediately upon seeing its twelve-character model number, but ninety-nine out of a hundred consumers do not. So, naming your products like this is selfish and self-serving—it benefits you while undermining your product development and marketing efforts. And, most inexcusably, it gets in the way of consumers' buying from you.
7. You are missing a huge product branding opportunity. You can't brand a fifteen-character product name for all of the reasons above.
8. These kinds of product names immediately and automatically cause your products to be perceived as commodities by consumers—even before launch. It's just another TV or digital camera if people can't refer to it in conversation.

9. They serve as a self-imposed hurdle that is all but impossible to overcome. Products with names like these cannot become singular products. They cannot develop passionate consumer fans because customers are prevented from remembering or referring to your devices. In the history of modern consumer electronics, a product with a name like this has never been viewed as singular and has never attracted consumer evangelists. Ever.

Your products are good. But the names you give them are among the first of a thousand cuts inflicted by the poor marketing that's so prevalent across the consumer electronics industry.

Industry Marketing vs. Evangelist Marketing: Kodak

➤ ➤ ➤

Industry Marketing

As of April 2011, here are some of the digital cameras Kodak lists on its Web site: the Kodak Easyshare M530, the Kodak Easyshare M532, the Kodak Easyshare M550, the Kodak Easyshare M552, the Kodak Easyshare M575, the Kodak Easyshare M580, the Kodak Easyshare M583, the Kodak Easyshare M580, and the Kodak Easyshare M590.

Evangelist Marketing

That's nine cameras between M530 and M590. They range in price from $80 to $200, from 12 megapixels to 14, from 3× optical zoom to 8×; they come in a variety of shapes, sizes, and colors.

Kodak's Easyshare brand is effective—it conveys the emotion of enjoying pictures with family and friends. But the model numbers don't tell us anything about these cameras. Worse, they hinder consumers from being able to identify, refer to, and describe their camera to others. Why not simplify the names? (When in doubt, always simplify your marketing.)

I would simply give these cameras a one-number product number: the Kodak Easyshare 3, the Kodak Easyshare 6. If necessary add a color: the Kodak Easyshare 4 in Red. It's how Apple does it with the iPhone, and how Amazon does it with the Kindle, and it seems to work for them.

The culture in marketing technology is to make things unnecessarily complex, and this often manifests itself particularly harmfully in your product names. Fight that urge and go simple instead. Almost 100 percent of the time, simple is better.

Who's Naming Your Devices?

This is happening across the industry because the wrong people are naming your products. I'm comfortable assuming that most of these names come from your engineers. That's because executives and (good) marketers would probably be incapable of creating such a garbled mess of outwardly meaningless letters and numbers that don't help consumers identify or understand your devices.

I was talking to a client recently who insisted that the name of their device—a computer accessory that all of us use every day—include all five words every time it's mentioned. My client kept saying, "That's how they want it." Unable to resist, I asked who are these mysterious people who name these products and insist that every one of the ill-conceived words be included with every mention of the device? The answer? "Legal."

Legal! Lawyers are naming this large, well-known company's multimillion dollar investments! Lawyers, who are trained to communicate in a way that is impossible for nonlawyers to understand. Lawyers, who overcomplicate simple matters on an hourly basis and charge for it. Lawyers, who can turn a one-page letter of agreement into a thirty-nine-page contract that takes three months to negotiate. In this company, lawyers, who are trained in law, not marketing or consumers or the retail marketplace, are responsible for undermining this company's every marketing activity because it now has to use a ridiculous, impossible-to-remember name with every reference to its functionally excellent devices. In this particular company, lawyers are screwing up the marketing. In other companies, it's the engineers.

You are asking consumers to learn your internal system and process for naming your devices. Imagine—not only are your customers worried about which product they are going to spend their hard-earned money on, but they must decipher countless naming systems. Is the 55 in ARLNC5560T for inches or storage capacity? Megahertz or megabytes?

"You Have to Give Products an Appealing Persona"

"Product names are really important—especially with handheld consumer electronics. In the mobile phone industry, these things are sensory extensions. They have eyes, skin, ears, mouths. You have to give them an appealing persona to the buyers, and a technical name doesn't do it. Linksys product names are terrible, I'm not afraid to admit that. That was born out of a very technical orientation within the company."

—Chris Dobrec, senior director, product marketing, Cisco Systems

Alex's Analysis: Consumer electronics are such a personal purchase. Even a Linksys router, the most technical product most people can buy at an electronics store, connects people to the Internet. It allows them to communicate with loved ones, wherever they may be. It brings them an infinite depth of information, entertainment, and productivity avenues. And yet, all people can remember about their router—from any company—is the manufacturer. The model is a mystery to most customers, making it impossible for people to remember and talk about your product.

The Names of the Most Successful Consumer Electronics

Now, let's look at another pattern. Consider these product names, widely regarded to be among the most successful, widely adopted, mainstream technologies of the last twenty years:

- The iPod (and before that, the Discman and the Walkman)
- The Mac®
- The iPhone
- The Motorola Droid
- The iPad
- Palm
- TiVo
- The Kindle
- Netflix
- Facebook
- The Blackberry

See the pattern? These names are short, crisp, memorable, sticky. They are easy to reference. They all pretty much use a single word as the product identifier. They're easy to say for consumers, and for the media, too. They're interesting.

Of course, the companies assign internally meaningful model numbers to these devices, but they are rarely, if ever, used publicly. In fact, it's hard to find any trace of Apple's model numbers on the company's Web site unless you really dig into Google to track it down. The MacBook® Pro 15-inch laptop, for example, has a model number of MC371LL/A, but you won't see that listed next to the product, because Apple is religious about not muddying the brand and awareness with such confusion. It's fine to go high-tech in your naming internally, but don't hang your internal vocabulary around consumers' necks by using it publicly. You're frustrating consumers and killing your sales.

Model numbers are so easy to get right. Just go simple. And yet, most manufacturers get it wrong, immediately damaging their chances for success in the market by hurting their marketing and public relations, and by turning off consumers. You're making countless unforced errors with your product names, setting yourself up for failure in an already incredibly competitive and challenging market. Selling consumer electronics is hard enough. Why do you voluntarily put yourself at a disadvantage before you even leave the gate?

This is too important. Get it right.

The Consumer Pricing Expectations Range (CPER)

Like a person going on a blind date, consumers have certain expectations when they go shopping for your products. Once shopping begins, these expectations fall into two categories: function and price. Functionally, people expect that your products will do what you promise, and the easier the better. So, consumers expect smartphones to make calls, access the Internet, take pictures, etc. High-definition televisions should have a good picture. Things should work as you say. This part is straightforward.

Their pricing expectations are similarly uncomplicated, but for some reason this issue trips up more than a few manufacturers. When it comes to your product costs, consumers expect your pricing will fall within a predetermined, acceptable range. They'll know immediately if a price feels too high or too low because they've been trained very well. By whom? By you: in your advertising, on your Web site, and in the Sunday newspaper advertising circulars. Your advertised pricing trains consumers about what to expect. Like children who can quickly solve the back-page puzzle in *Highlights* magazine, consumers know immediately which product's pricing "doesn't belong in this picture."

They know, for example, that a good point-and-shoot digital camera should not cost \$600. That's far too high. They also know that something's fishy when a camera is retailing for \$29. How good can it be? Consumers also know that a 50-inch flat-panel HDTV with a terrific picture should not cost \$3,000, no matter how many dimensions it displays. Unless Justin Timberlake and Peyton Manning walk out of that TV (for real, not just three-dimensionally), most people aren't going to pay \$3,000 for a TV today. Conversely, they would also wonder what's wrong with that HDTV if it costs \$149.

I call this the Consumer Pricing Expectations Range (CPER), and you'd best stay within it. There's no science to this: people know what the range is simply because the vast majority of the products in your category fall within it. If you're outside of the CPER, you're just giving people an easy reason to look elsewhere. This industry is fraught with hurdles as it is. It's very difficult to get new products to the mainstream, and once you do get customers, they're constantly being wooed by your competitors. Why give consumers another reason not to buy your products? There's so much competition out there. People have endless choices when buying any consumer technology.

The point is, this isn't complicated. Here's what the CPER model looks like. Stay in the sweet spot, and you eliminate an unnecessary, self-imposed problem:

FIGURE 5.1

The Consumer Pricing Expectations Range

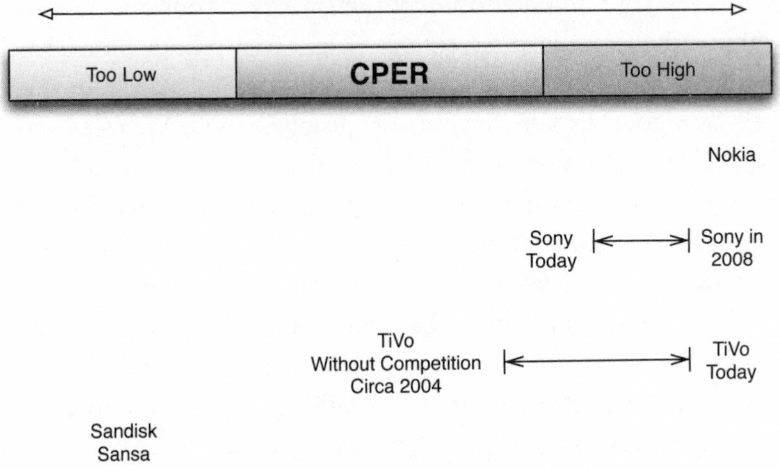

By default, most companies that have made it to the mainstream set the retail price of their products within the CPER. It is possible to adjust consumers' pricing expectations, but it's very, very difficult. Apple has done so, and Vizio has also. I'll address this a bit later. For now, let's look at some well-known companies that are laid out on the model above that have priced products outside the CPER.

Nokia: For many years now (which is an eternity in technology years), Nokia has been making excellent smartphones that have absolutely no chance to catch on with consumers because they are priced far higher than the competition. This is mostly because, unlike companies like Apple and Research in Motion, Nokia does not partner with wireless carriers who can subsidize the cost of their phones. When consumers can buy a new iPhone for $199 or get their hands on a number of Blackberry devices for free, Nokia's terrific devices don't stand a chance—not because they're functionally inferior but because their pricing is inferior. The company's top-of-the-line devices are often priced beyond $700. How can they possibly compete? Nokia's dissonant pricing is the single biggest reason it has lagged so far behind Apple, Research In Motion, and various Android smartphones in U.S. sales.

Sony: For most of the first ten years of this century, Sony's pricing was out of sync with the marketplace. Its Bravia televisions, although widely acknowledged to be among the best in the category functionally, often cost twice as much as other televisions. When consumers go shopping for an HDTV, and picture quality is similar (and by then, it was; most flat panels, even Sony's, are manufactured in only a few factories in Asia), they'll almost always go with the cheaper model. Similarly, Sony's PlayStation® 3 costs more than the two major competing consoles—the Xbox 360® and the wildly popular, motion-sensing Nintendo Wii. Guess which console brought up the rear in this three-way horse race for years, even though it was the most technically advanced unit? Yep, the PS3. Guess which model was the most affordable of the three? The Nintendo Wii, which also happened to lead the pack in sales for years.

Then, finally, in mid-2009, Sony realized its pricing was hurting its competitiveness. Bravia televisions came down in price dramatically and rather suddenly. The company also knocked off $100 on its PlayStation 3, bringing its cost more in line with the competition's. What do you think happened? Bravia took off almost immediately, and the PS3 leapfrogged the Xbox 360 and the Wii and became the top-selling video game console.

In Sony's case, by pricing its products much higher than consumers' expectations, pricing was the only obstacle to sales success. And it was self-imposed. As soon as they healed this self-inflicted wound and brought pricing within the CPER, sales took off—pretty much overnight. That's how important it is to price within the CPER.

TiVo: The first company to bring digital video recording to mainstream consumers once enjoyed evangelists. It had hugely passionate consumers; most of them felt that using TiVo not only changed their lives for the better but brought joy to their worlds. Because TiVo all but invented the DVR category, it was initially able to define its own CPER. That's why "TiVo without Competition" falls within the CPER sweet spot on the model.

But then cable companies like Comcast saw a huge opportunity for monthly revenue and started making their own DVRs. They packaged them with customers' existing monthly service. Although monthly service costs were initially similar (later, DVR service through cable and satellite companies was priced lower than TiVo's), it cost nothing to get a cable or satellite company's DVR. Through sheer muscle, television content providers redefined the CPER in the DVR category by providing them for free to millions of consumers. Even though their DVRs were functionally terrible at first (and, some would argue, still are today), especially when compared to TiVo's elegant, fun, feel-good interface, TiVo people switched when it was time to upgrade to a high-definition DVR. And people who never considered a DVR before got one because the risk was so low.

That left TiVo priced higher than the new market dominators, and suddenly on the high side of the CPER range. Since then, TiVo has been in survival mode. With little chance of mainstream consumer adoption due to its higher price, TiVo has been working on partnerships with cable and satellite providers for years with limited success.

Sandisk: Now let's look at a company that priced a terrific product below the CPER. In 2008, the flash memory maker Sandisk started marketing a product called the Sansa MP3 player. It's now widely available for around $30, significantly less than the competition's price. The most affordable iPod costs about $50. Sandisk has had a hard time selling the Sansa because it's priced below the CPER.

In addition to overcoming questions about how good an MP3 player from a memory maker can be, Sandisk has to deal with these questions:

- Why is the price so low?
- What is it missing?
- Is this too good to be true?

The Sansa is excellent. But the pricing is outside consumers' expectations, creating a problem where one would not exist if Sandisk priced the device higher.

Industry Marketing vs. Evangelist Marketing: Sandisk

➤➤➤

Industry Marketing

This is the product description on Sandisk's Web site for its Sansa Clip+ MP3 player:

> There's so much more to love when you play with a Sansa Clip+ MP3 player—for big sound and lots of features in a tiny package. Listen to up to 2,000 songs†† on your 8GB* player with amazing sound quality, FM radio, long-life battery, voice recorder and a memory card slot, too. And expand your fun indefinitely with slotRadio or slotMusic cards** preloaded with tunes ready to pop into the player's memory card slot

This player is priced at $70.

Evangelist Marketing

Sandisk has an interesting challenge on its hands here. Its $70 price is below the Consumer Pricing Expectations Range. Most people expect an 8GB MP3 player to cost $100 to $120, which is what Apple, the most successful maker of MP3 players, has taught the market. Sandisk would be wise to address this head-on, and, as with many companies in our industry, it wouldn't hurt Sandisk to go on offense a bit here. Here's how I'd do it:

> An 8GB MP3 player doesn't have to cost $120. Consider our $70 Clip+: it plays your music in amazingly high quality, includes an FM radio, a

CONTINUED ON FOLLOWING PAGE...

CONTINUED . . .

voice recorder, and even a memory card slot so you can expand the amount of music you can listen to. Most of the other MP3 players on the market don't have any of these extra features. So, we are offering unlimited music, radio, and voice recording for $80. The other guys are selling you eight gigabytes of music space for $120. Which would you rather have?

There is no shame in being aggressive when it's justified. And in this case, Sandisk would be wise to address people's concerns about their price head-on. This is a nice, preemptive way to do it.

Shifting the CPER

It's possible for a company to shift the CPER for its products, but it's very difficult. In other words, it's possible to price your products above or below consumers' expectations and still successfully sell them. To do so, you must have excellent marketing and extremely passionate consumers. Most companies in consumer electronics have neither, as we've already discussed. That is why most companies attempting to shift the CPER are not successful.

How Apple Raises the CPER

The only company that has successfully raised the CPER is Apple. As you can see, its range looks different from everybody else's. Apple devices almost always cost more than the competition's. Mac desktop and laptop computers cost more than nearly every other consumer computer. In fact, Macs are often twice the price of other computers. There is no price for Apple products—including Mac desktops and laptops, iPods, and peripherals like keyboards and mice—that is too high.

FIGURE 5.2

Apple's Consumer Pricing Expectations Range

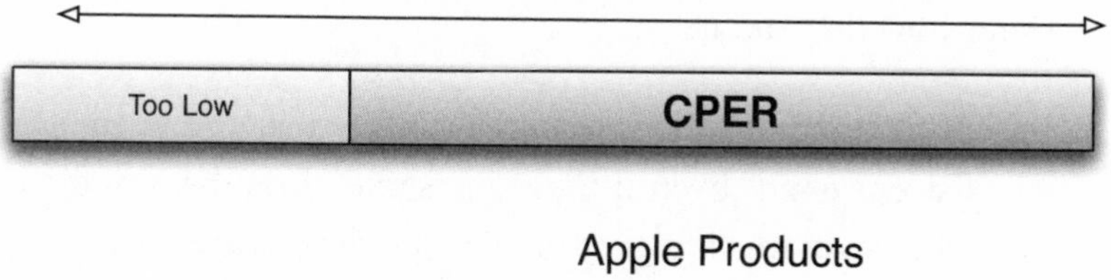

People expect Apple's products to cost more than the competition's. Apple has trained and prepared consumers for this by consistently rewarding them for paying a higher price with excellent devices that provide an incomparable experience. At least enough people believe this to make it so—that's really all that matters. People think they're getting an experience with an Apple device that they cannot get anywhere else. People feel good owning Apple devices. They love Apple. Apple almost never lets them down. And when they are let down, people generally don't hold Apple responsible. So, it's okay for Apple to price higher than the competition because it has spent decades developing consumers who are evangelists.

Vizio: Lowering the CPER

FIGURE 5.3

Vizio's Consumer Pricing Expectations Range

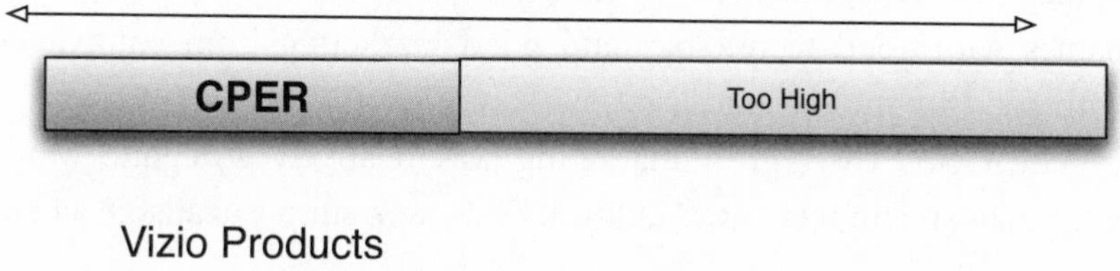

It's also possible to lower the CPER. That is, a few manufacturers have priced their products lower than most others, and have still sold a ton of units. One company that has successfully lowered the CPER in its category is Vizio, which started making televisions that cost much less than every other mainstream company's in the late 2000s. As you can see, Vizio's CPER also looks different than everyone else's. There is no price that is too low.

Here's how they did it:

- *They make excellent products.* Vizio's televisions are flat-out good. Even if they lack some of the bells and whistles of much higher-priced TVs, they have a terrific picture, which is why most people buy an HDTV.
- *They're widely and easily available at retail.* Vizio's popularity exploded when Wal-Mart started to carry its televisions. Then Sam's Club. Then Costco. Then the big Internet retailers. It was easy to buy Vizio TVs. In fact, before Vizio was available at technology retailers, it was sold at the discount chains.
- *And the big one:* It generated a lot of positive word of mouth. This is what separates Vizio from other companies that have unsuccessfully attempted to lower prices significantly below the industry average. People love their Vizio TVs, and they talk to each other about it. Every time we talked about HDTVs on my technology radio program, people called in to tout their Vizio TVs.

This is the major difference between Vizio and Sandisk, which has been less successful at lowering the CPER. Happy consumers did not generate enough word-of-mouth buzz about the Sansa MP3 player. There's a reason why I have "Word of Mouth" as the last step before "Consumer Evangelists" on my model. It's the step that separates companies with good technology and good marketing from companies with good technology and great marketing.

In Vizio's case, great marketing was relatively straightforward: huge mainstream retail availability. Its TVs were simply available where a lot of people shopped—and not necessarily for technology. So Vizio's breakthrough marketing step was getting its televisions on the shelves of large warehouse retailers. Success in our industry doesn't have to be complicated.

Why Wide Retail Availability Is Critical

This is one of the shortest sections in the book because it's such a straightforward concept. In order to succeed in the wildly competitive consumer electronics landscape, your products must be widely and easily available. Here's my definition of wide availability:

- Your product must be in the first or second place a consumer looks. Because they usually won't go to a third place.
- Your product must be intuitively available—the consumers shouldn't have to work to figure out where your device is available.
- Ideally, a Google search of your device should take consumers to a place where they can buy your product, rather than your Web site's product detail page.

Your product must be available in both the real world (Best Buy, Costco, Wal-Mart, Target, Staples, Kohl's, etc,) and online (amazon.com and buy.com). If customers are forced to look beyond these first-choice shopping locations, they will give up on looking for your product.

It's hard enough for consumers to navigate the technology landscape and figure out what to spend their hard-earned money on. Don't make them work to find your device once they've decided to buy your product. Make it easy for them.

Chapter Summary

The product names in our industry are unforgivably terrible.

- They are too long, too complicated, and too technical.
- They communicate little information to consumers.
- They make it impossible for consumers to remember, reference, and talk about your devices, which means they make it impossible for you to generate word of mouth.
- Your product names are undermining your multimillion-dollar products and your entire marketing and public relations effort.
- Successful product names are short, snappy, sticky, and brandable.
- Every one of the most successful products in modern consumer electronics history had a short, effective product name.
- Your product pricing must fall within consumers' expectations.
- Consumers' expectations are created by the industry—people are trained by the way in which most manufacturers price their devices.
- Price your products higher than the CPER, and people will not buy. They have too many better-priced alternatives.
- Price your products too low, and people will wonder what they lack. What's the catch? It is possible to shift the CPER higher but only if you have consumer evangelists and great marketing—extremely rare commodities in our industry.

part three

Consumer Insights

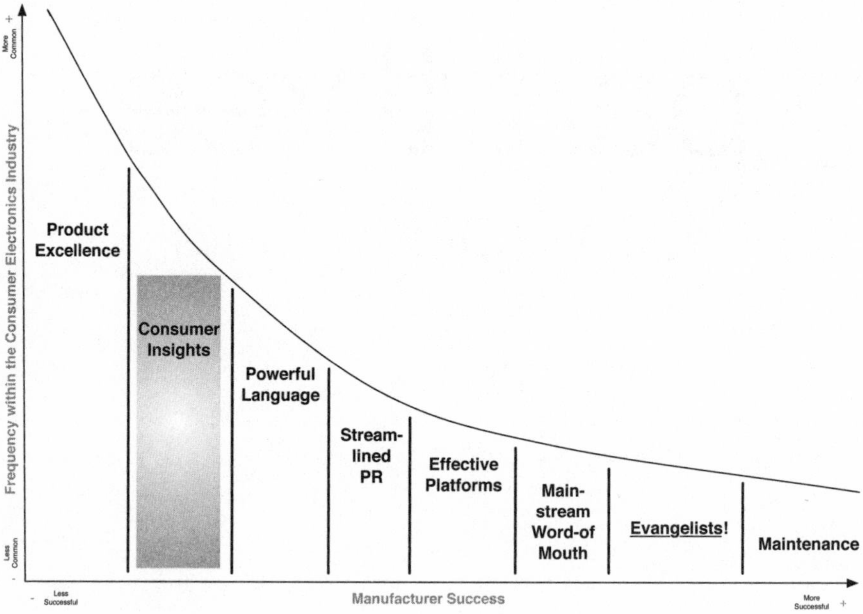
Frequency within the Consumer Electronics Industry
More Common +
- Less Common
Product Excellence
Consumer Insights
Powerful Language
Stream-lined PR
Effective Platforms
Main-stream Word-of Mouth
Evangelists!
Maintenance
- Less Successful
Manufacturer Success
More Successful +

six

Your Customers

You think you know your customers. Nearly all consumer electronics makers do.

The fact is, there's a range of customer information that most technology makers collect. You make serious efforts to learn certain kinds of information. It's what you're taught to collect in business school. Via online surveys, customer feedback forms, and the rare live conversations with your customers (aside from incoming customer service calls, how much do your people talk to your customers?), you learn your buyers' genders, age range, occupations, and income range. You learn whether they will use your product for business or personal use. You find out how they heard about your product. You ask where they bought it—online or offline, a big-box retailer or a specialty mom-and-pop shop.

This is useful information, and it's fine. It's the basics. But it's not nearly enough.

The fact that most consumer technology makers stop here—at the bare-bones basics—is a big underlying reason we have such poor marketing industry-wide. You don't communicate effectively with consumers because you don't know them well enough. Your marketing is lacking because you don't gather enough information. You don't have the necessary insights on your customers because you don't ask for them. There is so much more to know. So let's look at the kinds of customers that exist in consumer electronics.

Early Adopters vs. Mainstream Consumers

When startups in the consumer technology space come to market with a new product, they almost always begin by selling to early adopters. It makes sense, right? They're the low-hanging fruit, knowledgeable about new gadgets and willing to spend money to be among the first to try it. Early adopters also do a lot of talking, discussing their impressions, asking lots of questions about usage and functions, and sharing their experiences. They're almost an extension of beta testers, only the product is already shipping. Early adopters are fine, and they'll buy you some time, but they're obviously not the destination. You want mainstream consumers because they make up 95 percent or more of the market.

In his excellent book, *Crossing the Chasm*, Geoffrey Moore talks about the difficulty of crossing over from early adopters to mainstream consumers. The distance is the chasm. Using a bell curve model, he illustrates the chasm as the gap between what he calls the "early market" and the "mainstream market." I believe the distance between the two groups is significantly greater than Moore positions it, especially today, with the mind-numbing pace of technology development and product introductions. It takes a lot of time and effort to be an early adopter—both before the purchase (just staying on top of all the new product introductions—these folks must read *Engadget* and *Gizmodo* all day long—is a full-time job) and after the purchase (learning how to use these brand-new products, one after the other in rapid succession).

I think of the two groups as being on two different planets in the same universe. And space travel—your marketing in this metaphor—can rarely get you from the small, isolated planet to the big, interesting, highly profitable one.

FIGURE 6.1

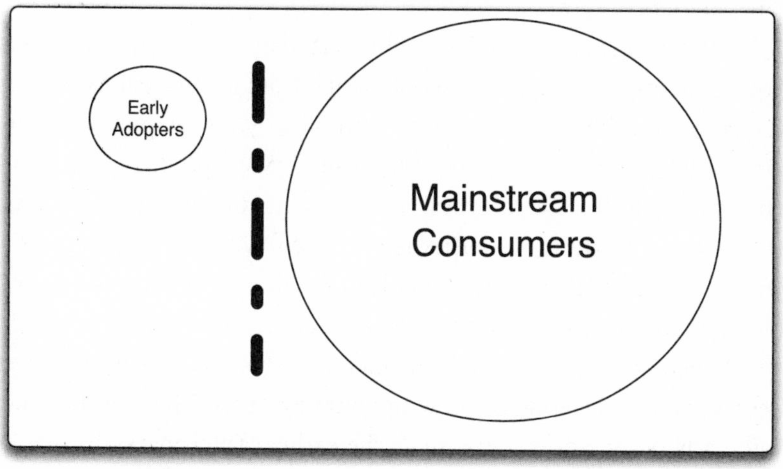

As you can see, it's possible to move from early adopters to mainstream consumers, but it's very difficult, and often has a lot to do with luck. The barrier between early adopters and mainstream consumers can be crossed, but the more you succeed with the more technical minority, the more difficult it becomes to cross over to the less technical majority.

The two groups require entirely different languages. You must speak technically to early adopters, but a focus on lifestyle and life improvement is necessary to get to the mainstream. They are receptive to different communications platforms as well: early adopters read blogs, message boards, and tech-related publications. Mainstream consumers do not—they consume more general-interest news.

One group doesn't really influence the other. Mainstream consumers can't understand what early adopters are saying, and early adopters couldn't care less what the mainstream thinks or does. They just want the latest and greatest.

As you master the early adopter market, you create internal habits that are very difficult to break. That is, your internal people become used to communicating using technical jargon and you master the marketing techniques that work with the technical minority.

Similarly, you train your channels about your products and your target audience.

So what's the problem? The problem is that mainstream consumers require a completely different set of habits, from language to platforms to channels and even distribution. And all of your people, internally and at the agencies, have learned to position your products and company successfully to tech types. These habits and processes become rooted very quickly because they're successful with the intended audience. But they're incredibly difficult to break and the transition from talking to tech types to talking to mainstream consumers can be tough.

Remember, your people's instinct is to use technical language. Messages and marketing begin with your engineers. They set the tone. And, early on, it works. Only, once the early adopter market is quickly saturated with your message and product, then what? You need to make the transition to the mainstream; you need to travel to the bigger and better planet. And it's nearly impossible to make that transition, to turn on a dime—or even over many months (which is far too long of course, especially in our industry). Many startups and new products from well-known brands have died almost immediately after having success with early adopters.

Therefore, I recommend you pass over early adopters entirely—don't even land on that planet—and go straight to the mainstream. *Make the mainstream your early adopters. Target them first.* This way, your language, marketing techniques, and communications platforms are formed and instituted to reach 95 percent of your buying public at the outset, instead of the 5 percent tech minority. You form habits to reach the right people from the very beginning. You train your channel partners about your real target customer. So the fruit hangs a little bit higher, but there is infinitely more of it.

The Customers You Create

The kinds of customers you create are a direct function of the interaction of your product excellence and your marketing excellence.

FIGURE 6.2

The Customers You Create

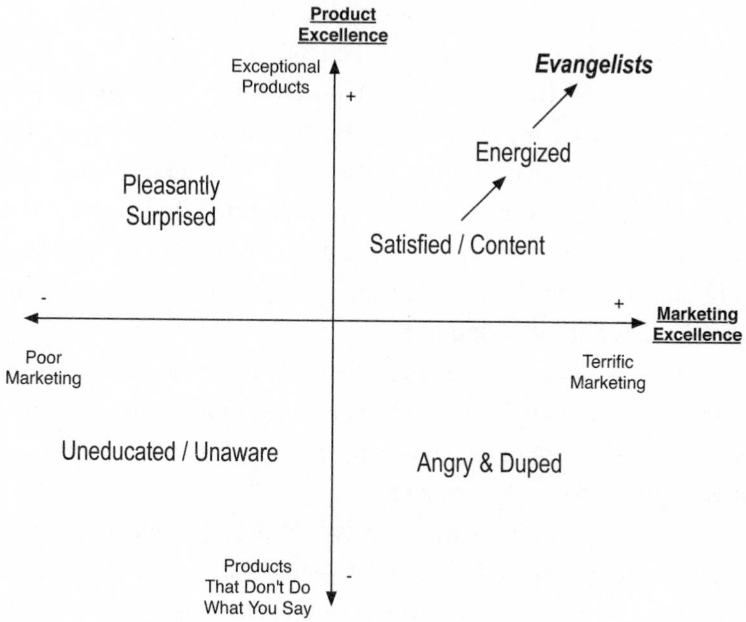

Let's move through the visual from the diagram from negative to exceptional.

Uneducated/Unaware Customers

If you have poor marketing and poor products, you have what I call uneducated or unaware customers. You don't have many customers, and even the ones you have will not be your customers for very long. Obviously, poor products supported by bad marketing don't stick around on the market for very long. Sometimes, well-known technology brands put a dud out onto the mainstream market. This is mostly the result of a series of breakdowns in the natural "poor product defenses" that consumers normally enjoy. Except this time, the manufacturer didn't realize the product was terrible before going to market. Retail buyers agreed to carry the product because of a long-term relationship with the vendor (often buyers at major retail establishments will put the brakes on a bad product, even if it's from a major manufacturer), the product made it to store shelves—online or offline, and the consumer happened to be among the first to buy it. They'd have to be among the first because bad products have short life expectancies once the returns and complaints begin coming in to the retailers.

A product like this ends up with few customers because the product is little known: consumers hadn't heard of it before deciding to buy it, making it somewhat of an impulse buy. There aren't many media reviews because the manufacturer hasn't submitted the product. There aren't many user reviews because it's early in the product's shelf life. Basically, consumers are prevented from doing their homework because there isn't much information to be had.

As a group, these customers aren't really angry because they don't give the product enough time or attention to get angry. Also, a critical mass of negativity does not build up because customers wash their hands of these products so quickly.

It doesn't take more than a few days of product ownership before the unaware consumers quickly learn—and teach!—exactly how bad this product is. They generate the reviews. They alert retailers by returning it in droves. After this first, intense wave of consumer feedback, the product doesn't have long left. The manufacturer is embarrassed, and has to pull the device quickly. And today, with *Engadget*, *Gizmodo*, *Mashable*, and countless other tech news sources observing the industry under a microscope, you cannot fail quietly. And you know who scours the popular specialty consumer technology sites, don't you? Not only early adopters or interested industry observers but mainstream news organizations as well. Your spectacular product failure will likely make it to the mainstream news in some form.

Best to avoid this quadrant.

Angry and Duped Customers

If your marketing is terrific and your products are not, your customers will be angry. They will feel like you have tricked them. These kinds of customers are rarely seen anymore because, as I've discussed previously, consumer electronics sold on the mainstream market today are generally very good. For years, however, consumers perceived Microsoft products as poor products with decent marketing. Remember, the Dells and Hewlett-Packards and Gateways of the world put out a ton of marketing back then. They competed with each other, and plastered newspapers and magazines with PC ads. For a time, the back of every magazine in America was a fold-out Dell ad with tiny print and fascinating pictures of dark computer cases.

From the late 1990s through the mid-2000s, our nation was filled with disgruntled Microsoft PC users. If you had a PC, you had Microsoft software on it. And if you had Microsoft software, you also had security issues, as well as freezing-crashing-control-alt-delete issues. Customers were angry about their Microsoft experience—they had paid good money to deal with these frustrations—but there were no real alternatives. And back then, many PCs cost more than $1,000, and they were a major, long-term purchase. (Today's powerful $300 computers are more easily replaced.)

Then, a few things happened to improve the atmosphere for Microsoft:

- The software improved. Windows just got better. To its credit, Microsoft realized it couldn't have the public encumbered with constant problems. So, it got safer, more secure, less prone to freeze.
- The advent of affordable consumer Internet access allowed Microsoft to distribute fixes as problems arose. Microsoft fixed the problems.
- The public perceived Microsoft to be working on the issues. They were seen as hustling. This helped a great deal.
- Alternatives arose. Thanks to the wildly popular iPod, followed up by the wildly popular iPhone, Mac computers became a real option for consumers.
- Cloud-based options arose. In the late 2000s, desktop-based software lost its viselike grip on the PC. Google apps became alternatives to Microsoft Office. Major

manufacturers like Acer started selling netbooks running the Linux operating system.

With more options, consumers no longer felt trapped by Microsoft. This reduced the level of vitriol. (I don't know if you remember, but there was a time when public sentiment toward Microsoft was very ugly.) Microsoft finally—finally!—began to market effectively. The company's 2010 ads that showed young, hip, happy people going into a big-box consumer electronics store and buying a low-cost PC, declaring, "I'm a PC," were the first truly excellent consumer marketing activities Microsoft had ever executed. I read that last sentence several times, and it really is what I wanted to write: it was Microsoft's first really powerful consumer marketing ever.

You can see how difficult it is to break out of this quadrant. And you can see also how many of the events involved in Microsoft's "escape" from this quadrant were really outside of the company's immediate control. Things developed in the industry. Technology lurched away from desktop computing toward cloud computing. The competition advanced. Microsoft's market share fell, and its grip on control of the desktop computer unraveled. And, in the end, when looking back at all that happened, Microsoft benefited, even from events that initially seemed damaging to the company.

The point is, you don't want to get stuck in this quadrant any more than you want anything to do with the quadrant that creates uneducated and unaware consumers. Consumers who feel angry and duped will pound you mercilessly.

You want to be in one of the upper two quadrants.

Pleasantly Surprised Customers

If you make functionally excellent products, but you're not very good at reaching and communicating that to consumers, you'll find yourself with pleasantly surprised customers. The majority of technology makers are here—making solid technology, and supporting it with poor marketing and communications.

So what's wrong with pleasant surprise?

It doesn't stick.

Pleasantly surprised consumers lack the energy and passion to drive your products within their inner circle. They view your product as a commodity and as easily replaceable. The thinking goes: *If I didn't buy this TV, that one would have probably been just as good.* Here's the biggest problem with consumers who are "only" pleasantly surprised: there's little commitment to your brand. Even if your television—or digital camera, or computer, or whatever—works flawlessly for them for years, these people will rarely go back to the store looking for a replacement device from your company. Any brand will suffice for them. If you're the outgoing brand, and your competition has a highly ranked product that's well reviewed and you do not, you don't stand a chance with these consumers.

Here are some more characteristics of these "pleasantly surprised" consumers:

- They are pleased but not committed.
- They are satisfied but not enough to communicate their satisfaction to others.
- Your product has met their basic requirements—but has not dramatically exceeded them. So what's the "surprise" then? These people expected to be let down. They hadn't heard much about your product before buying it, remember? You weren't talking to them effectively. So these folks come in prepared for disappointment.
- They're happy enough, but they're far from excited.

Read this list again. What a shame that an industry as creative and visionary—not to mention financially rich—as ours has more of these kinds of customers than any other kind.

Satisfied/Content, Energized, and Evangelist Customers

The customers in this quadrant are the result of excellent products supported by great marketing. These are the most desirable kind of consumers. As you can see, I've laid out three types of consumers here because excellence must be carefully detailed. In order of increasing energy, passion, commitment, trust, and strength of manufacturer relationship, the most desirable customer types are: satisfied, energized, and evangelist consumers. Better products (as laid out in Chapter 4) supported by better marketing end up creating more desirable customers.

The most successful products have the complete range of the customers in this quadrant. The iPhone, iPad, Amazon Kindle, and Netflix are singular products, and they enjoy customers who span the entire range. Some of their consumers are content. Some are energized. And some are evangelists. Companies that make special products, like Android device makers, conversely, only make it to the energized consumer level. These products do not have a critical mass of evangelists because they are not perceived at the same level as the iPhone, which is seen as singular. Some commodities do cross over into the satisfied/content part of this quadrant. These products typically put out somewhat better marketing than their counterparts, who max out with only pleasantly surprised customers.

Satisfied consumers:

- Generally view products as a commodity.
- Are pleased with product functionality and support.
- Are people who have heard about your product before beginning their shopping. The marketing in this quadrant is better, so the messages reach farther.
- Are more committed to your brand than pleasantly surprised consumers.
- Have more of a relationship with your company than pleasantly surprised consumers.
- Are more willing to continue buying your brand when it comes time to replace their current product.
- Are not quite as interested in what other products you're making. For example, people are generally satisfied and content with their Samsung HDTVs (as well as their LG and Sony HDTVs), but they don't really care that their Blu-ray player is made by Samsung. That's because, as

much as they like your television, they still view it as a commodity. But Apple customers, who are far more energized and evangelistic, care greatly that their computer and their phone and their tablet is made by Apple. That's the difference.

Energized consumers:

- Generally view your products as special. You do not make commodities in these people's eyes.
- Are more passionate about your devices and your brand.
- Are extremely satisfied with their product experience.
- Were well aware of your products before they purchased them. They've heard their friends, family, and colleagues talking about your products.
- Create energy for your products and brand by talking about their positive experiences. They feel rewarded when they convince somebody else to purchase your device. Isn't that nice?

Evangelist consumers:

- Love your company.
- Love your products.
- Shout how much they love your devices from the mountaintops. These people spread your gospel.
- Seek out news and information about you.
- Surround themselves with like-minded evangelists. This is where communities like MacRumors get their energy.
- Make it their personal mission to enlighten others about your products.

Remember, you are responsible for the kinds of customers you develop: from the unaware customers to the angry ones to the energized and the evangelistic customers, you reap what you sow. If you make excellent products—and most of you do—and promote them with excellent marketing—and most of you do not—you will develop passionate, energized, and ultimately, evangelistic consumers. This is within your direct control. These customers don't happen to you. They are developed by you. The more desirable the customer type, the better your products and marketing must be.

The Customer Continuum

To illustrate the next couple of points, let's look at these customer types, as well as one additional type, along a continuum:

FIGURE 6.3

The Customer Continuum

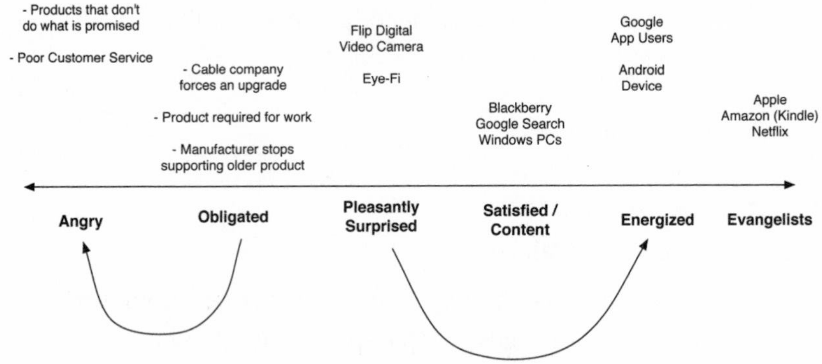

I've added a customer type here that doesn't fit on the double-axis chart from the last section: the obligated customer. Here are the characteristics of the obligated customer: they have purchased your product not out of need but because events conspired. Perhaps they must own your device because it has been mandated by their employer. Perhaps they have an older model that malfunctioned and is no longer being supported by the manufacturer—whether it's from your company or another one—and they must purchase a new device. Or perhaps they once had over-the-air standard definition television, and the bandwidth was overtaken by emergency service agencies, and their standard definition television suddenly became useless. They didn't want to buy the new product they just bought. They felt forced to do so. These customers are not happy. They had to part with money they did not want to spend.

As such, as you can see on the continuum, obligated customers can often become angry customers. It's an easy shift from feeling trapped into using a product to feeling angry about it.

It's important to note here that the customer continuum is fluid, with customers moving from one position to another. The only wall is between happy and unhappy customers. That is, once a customer is worked up enough to feel unhappy, let down, or duped by your product, there is little you can do to make that customer a happy one. This customer is pretty much lost to you. Conversely, a customer can easily go from somewhat unhappy to very unhappy. It wouldn't take much, but a frustrating customer service experience would make it happen quickly. Similarly, customers can move from slightly happy—or pleasantly surprised—to satisfied, to energized, and even to evangelistic if your actions warrant it.

I say "your actions" because moving a customer to the right on this continuum is entirely within your control. After they buy your product, their initial level of satisfaction is based on their experience with your product. But their movement up and down the continuum is dependent upon their experience with you. For example: How much support for the product is offered on your Web site? Are there videos and demonstrations? Is there an easy-to-access community of fellow customers that can offer tips, tricks, and techniques for using your product? Was the device easy to activate? How was their experience with your customer service people? All this turns a somewhat happy customer into a thrilled customer.

And as you can see on the continuum, consumers who are pleasantly surprised upon purchasing your products can jump straight to energized customers, and become part of your marketing team.

Customer Loyalty, Temptation, and the Greenest Grass

Like all complicated relationships, technology consumers deal with loyalty and temptation issues every day. Except, unlike friendships and marriage, in this industry, nothing is forever. Nothing is guaranteed. Even the most loyal customers switch companies, carriers, providers, and loyalties regularly. Sometimes it happens daily (Google lovers venturing over to Microsoft's Bing), and sometimes it happens biannually (when smartphone contracts run out). Sometimes it happens on a whim, when a sexy alternative cannot be resisted at the right price, and sometimes the courtship (research process) is long and drawn out.

In March 2010, a company called Crowd Science put out a fascinating look at smartphone loyalty. The results found that 40 percent of Blackberry users wanted an iPhone. Another third of these Blackberry owners would switch to an Android phone if they could. (I take the "if they could" to mean that they were attached to their Blackberry phone because it was mandated by their employers. These are obligated customers.) By comparison, nine of ten iPhone and Android users said they had no interest in switching.

Here's what's most interesting: many of those Blackberry users who felt themselves being wooed by the iPhone and various Android devices said they would not switch even if they could. They wanted to. But they would not. So Research in Motion was doing something right back then. I'll tell you precisely what they were doing right: RIM remained excellent—best of class—at what it was known for: email. People got Blackberry phones because they were great at sending and receiving email. And while all these sexy new phones tempted Blackberry users with their big touchscreens, their movies, and their massive app stores, people doubted—correctly—that their email experience would be as flawless as it was with their current device. It would be fine, maybe even very good. But it would not be "Blackberry great." These millions of Blackberry customers were so loyal to their device, to its manufacturer, that they passed up other, newer, more tempting, even sexier devices. They flirted. They studied. They might have even touched the new devices at the store. But they stayed true to what they knew worked for them. At least for the moment.

But the problem with consumer electronics is that there are "decision moments" frequently and regularly. For some people, it's daily. Perhaps they take the train to work and see people using iPhones and Android devices. Or maybe they're technology news junkies and are constantly seeing stories about these other smartphones. But every time a new product launches in your category, it has the ability to catch your customer's eye. Will that grass look greener? Your job is to make that grass look unattractive by making your grass the greenest in the category neighborhood. More on green grass shortly, but for now, let's look at two uncomfortable industry truths that the results of this survey shine a light on.

Keeping Customers Is More Challenging Than Ever

Keeping a customer using your device is more challenging than ever. Your job is to keep emphasizing and improving your competitive advantage. People bought your products for some main reason. You must know that reason, and you must constantly work on improving it. Think about how Netflix keeps increasing the selection of movies and devices through which its service is available. Think about how Apple keeps improving iPhone and iPad operating systems, for free, to existing customers. Think about the app store, which allows for new improvements to an older device. Improve on the reasons people came to you in the first place.

You must never stop marketing, especially to your existing customers. Because they'll leave you in three seconds if you rest on your laurels.

Talk to your customers every day. Have executives get on the phone with them. Let engineers hear from the human beings who use the products they create. Find out what people like about your devices, how they are using them, and what they like and dislike most. Forget about the invaluable information you'll learn: imagine how impressed your customers will be to pick up the phone and hear, "Hello, Mr. Smith, my name is Mark and I was on the team that invented your current smartphone. If you don't mind, I'd love to talk to with you for five minutes about what you like and don't like about your phone." Leave that in a voice mail, and, after the shock wears off, you'll get a call back nine times out of ten.

Home Products

And yet, once a customer finds a good "home" within a consumer electronics category, it's quite difficult to lure him away. I define a "home product" as a technology that brings the consumer pleasure and that the consumer has grown dependent on and to which he or she is committed.

The leading smartphones—the iPhone, the Blackberry, and the numerous Android phones—are considered home devices by many consumers. This occurs in part because these devices connect us to home when we are far away. Also, people make a commitment to a smartphone platform and experience. They learn the ins and outs of a device they interact with as many as hundreds of times per day.

Netflix is a "home" technology. Once customers experience Netflix, they rarely go to a competitor. Netflix brings joy and entertainment to consumers, across numerous devices at home and while away.

The Kindle is a home product—few people switch from it.

Once a customer finds a "home product," you're going to have a hellish time luring that customer away—even if you argue that your product is better, more affordable, or easier to use. The consumer is attached to their home product. They're devoted to it. Or, less positively, they feel stuck to it. If a customer has eighteen months remaining on their Verizon Wireless contract, it's unlikely they're going to come to AT&T no matter how hard AT&T tries to win them.

Work on doing everything you can to make your device a "home device." How do you do that? Improve your product and improve your marketing. For details, finish reading this book!

On Building Relationships with Consumers Without Two-Year Contracts

❖ ❖ ❖

Virgin Mobile only sells month-to-month, prepaid plans.

> "For the wireless companies, it's an orientation to herding to the franchise, but not necessarily taking care of customers, building a relationship. It's really about monetizing it. Then at month twenty or twenty-one it becomes about talking to those customers. For us, it's really about let's get them in, and let's inspire them. We're not going to use technology language. We're going to have conversations with them, and the conversation is not going to stop once we have them as a customer. We're going to help them understand the relationship they're in. 'You're valuable to us, we're going to intro a new handset, what do you think about these names we're going to consider. What do you think?' Let's define the relationship we want to build long term with customers."
>
> —Bob Stohrer, vice president of marketing, Virgin Mobile

Alex's Analysis: Bob needs to develop these relationships with his customers because Virgin Mobile is one of the only large wireless carriers in America that doesn't lock consumers into two-year contracts. There is no lock and key, no financial penalty keeping people with Virgin Mobile. The only way the company

CONTINUED ON FOLLOWING PAGE…

CONTINUED . . .

can keep its customers is by making them very happy. Every product manufacturer in the industry is in this boat. What kind of relationships do you have with your customers? What kind of relationships have been defined as ideal? And what are you doing to create and maintain them?

Back to Green Grass

A quick story: at our home, we once hired a national grass fertilization outfit that didn't cost very much. We wanted greener grass and fewer weeds, and this company's service seemed like a quick solution. After one treatment, we saw no improvement. After a second application of their "fertilizer," my lawn started to disappear in patches. I called them, and they figured the solution was to throw some more chemicals on the grass. A couple weeks later, large parts of our lawn had degenerated into empty dirt. Our lawn looked like an overused soccer field. I called again, and without any resistance, they sent a different machine to reseed my lawn, in an effort to fix their damage.

After this experience, I stayed away from grass treatment companies for several years. The reseeding worked fine, and I decided I could live with the weeds, which were better than brown, dusty patches. Well, recently the dandelions got particularly bad, and I started researching fertilizer companies again. This time, I went with a small, family-owned local organization. They had studied our area's grass makeup with professors from the local universities, and devised the treatment compound in concert with these professors. They had to come back repeatedly to treat the weeds but only charged me for one application.

After one summer of their work, my grass had never looked better. They created incredibly thick, green, lush grass.

That first company, the national outfit that burned out my lawn, that's analogous to the marketing campaigns of most manufacturers in the consumer electronics industry. You generally do the same things everywhere, consistently ineffectively, without much insight about the target or its needs. The second company, which won my business for as long as they decide to stay operational, is analogous to the best marketers in the business: Apple, Amazon, and Netflix. They knew their target—my grass—extremely well. They had insights based on deep research. They tailored their delivery based on this knowledge. They obliterate the competition because they build such loyalty in their customers that going elsewhere is never even a real option. What a massive achievement in today's wildly competitive consumer electronics market: going elsewhere isn't even considered.

That's your job: to create the greenest grass for your customers. You build loyalty by having exceptional products and great marketing—before and after the sale. You also build loyalty by finding ways to improve your product or service while the consumer owns it. Built-in expansion is a huge shared characteristic among the very best technologies.

Consumer electronics customers are constantly being tempted. The stronger your relationship is with them, the greater the chance that they will stick with you instead of the newer, trendier, sexier competition.

Like the rest of the techniques in this book, there's no magic here. Technology customer loyalty comes down to doing the disciplined work of gathering insights about your customers and then taking action based on what you learn about them.

Chapter Summary

You are directly responsible for the kinds of customers you create.

- The customers you create are a result of the interaction of product excellence and marketing excellence.

- Poor marketing combined with products that don't do what you say create uneducated, unaware customers.
- Poor products backed by excellent marketing make for customers who feel angry and duped.
- Bad marketing but excellent products create consumers who are pleasantly surprised at the quality of your offerings.
- And good marketing and products create a continuum of consumers who can be satisfied or content, energized, and evangelistic.

There is another sort of consumer, who feels trapped into using a product he or she doesn't want to use. I call this customer "obligated."

Customer loyalty is fleeting—there are endless alternatives hitting the market constantly.

The exception to this rule is when consumers find a "product home"—that is, a product or service they commit to.

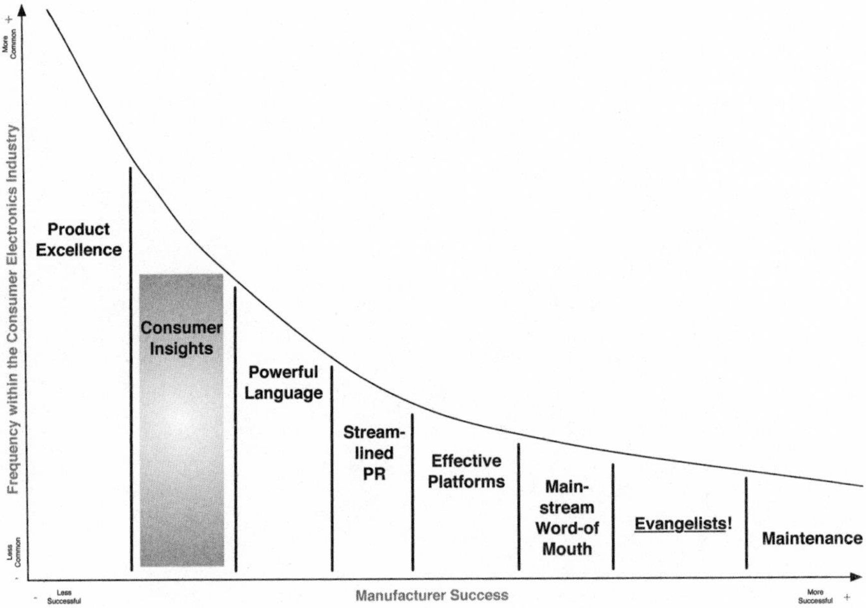
Frequency within the Consumer Electronics Industry
More Common +
- Less Common
Product Excellence
Consumer Insights
Powerful Language
Stream-lined PR
Effective Platforms
Main-stream Word-of Mouth
Evangelists!
Maintenance
Manufacturer Success
- Less Successful
More Successful +

seven

Everything Begins with Consumer Insights

There's a massive problem in the consumer electronics business. This problem plays a huge role in all that is wrong with the marketing in our industry. It is occurring in the vast majority of companies making electronics today. It costs many consumer technology companies millions of dollars, and others lose billions annually as a direct result of it. This problem is as shocking as it is inexcusable. It is also incredibly simple to fix; you just have to decide to fix it. The work involved in solving this problem is not difficult, and doesn't really take a lot of time. In fact, it's rather enlightening and interesting work. This is the problem: most consumer electronics companies don't know what their consumers want from, think about, or do with their products.

What?! How can that be? You spend millions on industry research. You conduct huge surveys or pay professionals to read the results of their studies. You poll your customers. You offer discounts or perks for consumers to answer your questions. You ask them where they heard about your products. You know if they use your technologies for personal or professional reasons. You've learned where they bought your product—which store, which state, which Web site, etc. You know the name of their employer. You have their email address and their mailing address. You conduct focus groups and watch them use your products in a group setting. You ask them questions about their experience at that focus group. You get their feedback in a group setting.

But you don't know what your customers *want* from your products. And you don't know how they *think* about your devices. And you don't know how they really *use* your devices when they're at home, without a group or a two-way mirror.

You might think you do, but most of you don't.

And you don't know because you don't ask. Our industry almost never talks to consumers one-on-one about their thoughts and feelings and wishes for our technology.

And so without this critical baseline information, your product managers, most of whom have an engineering background, dream up new products based on technical specifications. You try to out-speed, out-store, out-big, and out-impress the competition. You think about how to get better placement on the shelf at retail, and how to get the online sellers to promote your devices over the other guys'. You go technical by default because that's what your competition is doing. You don't know what consumers want, think, or do, so you assume. And the people doing the assuming happen to be the product managers, who are dreaming up your products.

Let me say it differently: the people (incorrectly) assuming that consumers are intensely interested in technical specifications have an immediate influence on your research and development spend (many millions), your product development (also many millions), and intricate marketing and public relations campaigns (do I even need to say it?), based on incorrect messages and language. In other words, not talking to consumers is a wildly expensive and destructive problem in consumer electronics.

It's at the root of the marketing problems in our industry.

Industry Marketing vs. Evangelist Marketing: Tom-Tom

➤ ➤ ➤

Industry Marketing

Here is the first paragraph of the product description of Tom-Tom's XL-340TM GPS—which is a fine device:

> Get street smart with the TomTom XL 340TM—complete widescreen navigation, featuring Lifetime Traffic and Map Updates. Outsmart traffic and minimize delays with Lifetime Traffic Updates. Based on incoming traffic events, your device will suggest alternate routes. And, with Lifetime Map Updates you'll always drive with the latest and most accurate maps. On average, 15% of the road network changes each year, so it is important to have the most up-to-date maps. With the XL 340TM you'll always stay current.

Evangelist Marketing

Although the name may not be reasonable, the information in the descriptive paragraph above is—these are great functionalities. But the focus is very much on the product and its features, and not on the consumer. Remember, this is the first paragraph in the product description. It must capture consumers. Here's how I'd translate this to address consumers' emotions:

> The TomTom XL 340TM will get you where you're going faster. It'll take you around traffic, so you can spend more time with your family. In addition to a lifetime of live traffic updates, you

CONTINUED ON FOLLOWING PAGE...

CONTINUED . . .

also get free map updates. New construction? New roads? No problem. The TomTom XL 340TM is always current, and always loaded with the most recent maps available. So you can get in your car knowing TomTom will get you where you're going safely, quickly, and dependably.

My paragraph gets the same information across as the company's. But it focuses on the customer's life, and what's important to him. If you talked with 100 Tom-Tom customers, I'd bet the words *safe*, *dependable*, *updated*, and *traffic* would come up a lot. Addressing customers' emotions is always more powerful than listing features.

Imagine the Unimaginable: Talking to Your Customers

I want to define what I mean by talking to consumers. I mean engaging in one-on-one qualitative conversations with your customers. I don't mean quantitative research, so talking to your consumers does not include research that asks thousands of people the same three questions. My definition of talking to your customers does not include online surveys. It does not include focus groups, where answers and behaviors are affected and influenced by the others sitting in the room. Talking to consumers does not mean the five answers people provide during product registration. And technical support conversations don't fit into my definition either.

My technique for talking to your customers revolves around actually talking to your customers. Because this is not something that most of you engage in, here are six defining characteristics of effective consumer conversations:

- Talking to your customers means picking up the phone. The most valuable information during these conversations is often uncovered with a series of follow-up questions, which means that talking to your consumers is most effectively done over the phone. Don't use email. Or those horrific, never-ending online surveys that have come into vogue lately. You want to be able to ask questions, listen to the answers, and then follow up as needed. You want to go where the consumer is taking you. This is only possible in personal conversations. And because you're keeping them brief, consumers will be more inclined to participate in these interviews, as opposed to the thirty-five-page questionnaire.
- These conversations should not be handled by dedicated staff. Don't hire people to do this. Have your employees do it, and I mean everyone. Executives. Managers. Secretaries. Guess who you want talking to customers more than any other group? That's right, your engineers and product managers. These folks have incredible technical minds, but few of them ever deal with people who use their creations in the real world. This is the major disconnect between technology makers and your customers. My technique of customer conversations bridges that gap. Get your people talking to the people who keep you in business.
- Conversations should last no more than fifteen minutes. In fact, ten minutes is usually enough. In the next sections, I'll provide the questions you want answered, and you'll be able to create your own custom script for this.
- No more than one conversation per day per employee. Imagine if each of the people in your company talked to one consumer per day. Imagine how much more effective they would be in their jobs. Imagine the great insights they'd gather about how their work—and your company's products—affect the lives of real people.

- Log the results into a standardized database. I'm sure you'll figure out the technology (it's what you're good at!), but any tool will do. Have your staff log your consumers' replies and experiences. The idea is that you are creating a collection of customer case studies. How powerful is that?
- Examine the case studies (conversations) for trends and consistencies. Although each conversation is extremely valuable on its own, the real power of this process is in the aggregate. A deeper discussion of your consumers' thoughts and experiences will become the foundation of your marketing and your messaging.

The value of doing this is nearly unlimited.

- You learn about what your consumers do with your products.
- You understand which features they use, and which ones they don't.
- You get insight into what your customers want and expect from you.
- You start to understand how people outside your company think about your products.
- You uncover the language people use to talk about your products. Listen to their words.
- And the big one: this technique is the most powerful, most effective way to market your products and your company. Why? Because, if you ask people the questions I lay out a bit later in this chapter, they will be telling you which marketing techniques to use, the messaging points to emphasize, the features that are the most important to them, and the exact language to use. All you need to do is collect these insights, process them, and then turn them right around onto the marketplace. Here is what this process looks like:

FIGURE 7.1

Consumer Insights

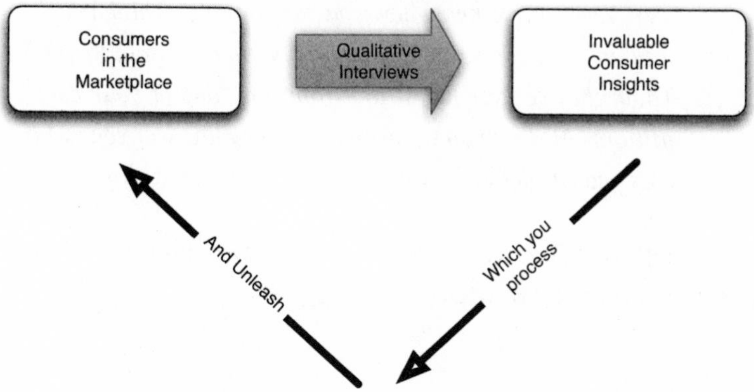

Objections

Why wouldn't you do this? What's preventing you from really talking to your customers? Here are some objections I've received from clients. My responses are in italics.

- We don't have the time. *Really? Fifteen minutes per day? Most of your people waste more than that on social media before lunch.*
- We don't have the people for this. *You have exactly the people for it. Start with your highest-level executives. Then your engineers and product managers. Then your marketers and public relations folks. Then your administrative and support staff. In reality, you have far more people for this than are necessary.*
- We don't know what to say. *I provide several scripts—and transcripts of actual conversations I've conducted with technology customers—in this chapter.*
- We don't have our customers' phone numbers. *You have some. Start with those. Then email the customers whose numbers you don't have. Tell them you'd like to have an*

executive or engineer call them for ten to fifteen minutes because their thoughts and experiences are so important to you. You'd be honored if they'd talk to you for a few minutes. You want to know how you can improve. Think people wouldn't respond to that? Think they wouldn't talk to you? Think they've ever heard that from any one of your competitors? Also, ask these customers if they know anyone who uses your devices who would be willing to talk with you.

The objections are weak. The value is overwhelming. And the time required is minimal. So, what's stopping you?

"It's a Question of Listening"

❖ ❖ ❖

"One of my favorite maxims is communication is not what you say, it's what someone hears. Fundamentally, it's not a question of speaking. It's a question of listening. Can you put together some communication so that someone hears it the way you want it to be heard?"

—Tony Lee, vice president of marketing, TiVo

Alex's Analysis: What's all but guaranteed to be heard by consumers the way you want it to be heard? The thoughts and experiences of other consumers. Your deep insights about your customers, if gathered, processed, and unleashed back upon consumers as communication have a far greater chance to be heard and acted upon in meaningful ways. The alternative is what's happening now: the language of your engineers, technical specifications. That becomes a guaranteed case of you speaking, and the consumer hearing nothing.

How to Gather Consumer Insights

The best way I know to obtain insights about customers is to ask for them. Here are ten questions to ask consumers for each of the three major areas for which you are seeking insights. Next to some of the questions, I'll detail the purpose of asking in parentheses. All of these questions assume that the customers you're speaking with are your customers. They went shopping. They compared available products. And they chose yours.

What Do Your Consumers WANT from You?

1. Why did you start shopping for this product? (This will uncover each consumer's reason for entering the market. This information is incredibly valuable for your marketing.)
2. What do you feel you were missing when you started shopping for this? What itch were you trying to scratch?
3. Which features were most important to you when you were shopping? (You'll learn which technical specifications were most important to consumers, so you can focus on them in your marketing and messaging.)
4. Which features or product capabilities stood out to you in our product when you bought it?
5. Now that you've owned and used it for a while, what's missing? What do you wish it could do?
6. How has your experience/interaction been with our company?
7. What's your one favorite gadget or technology item? In your mind, how do we compare to the company that makes that?
8. How can we improve?
9. What do you think we do best?

10. Why do you think your friends and family buy this type of product? (Trying to uncover consumer motivation. You're looking for people's feelings.)

How Do Your Customers USE Your Product?

1. Who uses our product in your home most? Is there anyone else besides you who uses the device?
2. How do you use the device? (Begin with general questions. Open-ended questions are more effective at the beginning of these conversations because you are not creating confines around where people can take their answer. Where they go will reveal a great deal about what's important to them.)
3. What do they (you) do with the product most? Why? (Now you can begin asking more specific questions, looking to address certain areas of your marketing and communications.)
4. Which parts of the device do you not put to use?
5. Why do you think you avoid those functionalities?
6. What are your favorite features?
7. Where do you use our product most? If at home, where specifically? If outside of the house, where?
8. Who are you typically with when using our device?
9. What are you normally doing when using the product? (Driving? Resting? Working?)
10. Which feature was the greatest surprise to you when you started using our product? (This will shine a light on a product functionality that you are probably not talking about. If enough people say the same things, you'll have a powerful new marketing point to communicate to the public.)

How Do People THINK About Your Products?

1. When you think about our style of device (by this, I mean your product category: HDTV, camera, computer, phone, etc.), what are the first words that come to mind?
2. What does this product do for you?
3. How does it improve your life?
4. How does it improve your family's life?
5. When you talk about our device to others, what do you say?
6. Can you sum up your thoughts about our device in one sentence?
7. Describe our device in just three words.
8. How does our product make you feel?
9. If you had to teach your mother about our product, how would you do it?
10. What's the most powerful, accurate thing we can say about this product?

* Bonus Question: How did we do in educating you about our device before you bought it?

* Bonus Question 2: If you were us, what would you say about this product to excite your peers?

How to Use These Questions

I put this list of questions together to get you started. You should not be asking every customer you interview every one of these questions. You'll lose people quickly. Rather, ask people at least one or two from each of the three categories, and ask follow-up questions as needed. And feel free to add your questions, of course. The idea is to dig in. You're looking for thinking, motivations, desires, and language. You are obtaining points of emphasis for your future marketing, as well as the actual words to use in your communications. But be sure you leave yourself the flexibility to go where the consumers are taking you. Don't fight them if they begin talking about an area you feel is not one of your priorities going into the conversation. The key is, it's a priority to the person with whom you're talking. If what this person says is interesting to you, you can ask the next person about it. Maybe you even add it to your list of questions. Stay agile and open-minded. And, after ten minutes are up, let the person know that being respectful of his or her time is important to you, and your prearranged ten-minute timeframe is up. My experience is that nine out of ten people will happily continue until they have said what they want to say, regardless of timing.

Sample Conversations with Customers

Here are three sample conversations for three different categories of consumer electronics. To illustrate the various ways these conversations can go, demonstrate the kinds of insights you will uncover, as well as preserve client confidentiality and consumer privacy, these are not transcripts of real conversations. Rather, they are based on real interviews that I—and my clients—have conducted with consumers.

For a Smartphone

YOU: Why were you shopping for a smartphone?

FEMALE CONSUMER: I wanted one thing that would make calls, do my email, and browse the Internet. Oh, and take some pictures and play some games, too.

YOU: Why pictures and games?

FEMALE CONSUMER: Well, I really wanted to take pictures of my kids. And I like to have fun, too. Life isn't all about work, you know!

YOU: OK, if it's alright with you, I'd like to talk to you about each of those areas. Talk to me about taking pictures of your kids with our phone. How has that worked out for you?

FEMALE CONSUMER: It has been awesome. I love being able to shoot and share so many pictures throughout the day. When my husband is traveling, I send them to him. My parents live out of state, and I feel like I've been sending them pictures of the kids every day! Oh, and I'm actually using the video recording a lot more than I thought.

YOU: Did you know our smartphone records high-definition video before you bought it?

FEMALE CONSUMER: No. I didn't. But now I love it.

YOU: Love is a strong word. Why do you love it?

FEMALE CONSUMER: Because I'm not very technical, and I feel like our camcorder is really complicated to use. This video camera is on my phone. How cool is that! And it's really good quality, and then I just email it to my parents.

YOU: Is that your favorite feature?

FEMALE CONSUMER: Definitely. The video and the photos.

YOU: Earlier, you mentioned games, and how it was fun for you to play.

FEMALE CONSUMER: Love the games! How fun is Angry Birds?! Sometimes I like to disconnect and play for five minutes. Or just two. Or when I'm waiting for a phone call to start.

YOU: Were you a gamer before getting our product?

FEMALE CONSUMER: No. Not even close. I couldn't play a PlayStation or Wii box if my life depended on it.

YOU: So if you had to describe how our smartphone has improved your life, how would you do it?

FEMALE CONSUMER: Well, just thinking about our conversation, I'd say I take far more photos than I ever have, I record videos, and I relax with the games. I mean, I'm recording my kids growing up here. And then the same product also lets me play and have fun. Oh, and I can call, email, and text, too. It's incredible.

YOU: Let's narrow it down a bit: If you had to use three words to describe the phone, what would those words be?

FEMALE CONSUMER: Incredible. Fun. Relaxing.

YOU: If you were selling this phone, what would you say about the phone to communicate what it can do most effectively?

FEMALE CONSUMER: I'd talk up the camera and video camera WAY more. You guys just assume that we know these things. And I guess I knew the phone had a camera on it when I bought it. But I had no idea how good it was. Or how much I'd use it. Or how easy it was to record videos of my kids. I wish I would have known these things. I would have bought it a lot sooner.

And wrap.

I've heard countless consumers talk about how wildly underemphasized the camera and video camera features are on smartphones. See, to the engineers and product managers who determine what your company will say about your technology to the world, many features that consumers find incredibly valuable are old news. It's just another part of the huge disconnect between the people making your products—and defining your marketing—and the people you are trying to teach about your products.

So, what did you learn from this conversation about smartphones? That emphasizing the camera and video functionality of your smartphone would probably be smart to do. That this consumer used the words *incredible*, *fun*, and *relaxing* to describe your phone. Are you using those words? Those are pretty good words. Think it would be powerful to say, "Our customers say our phones are incredible, fun, and relaxing"? Of course, you're going to compare this customer's insights with those from a number of others, but this one ten-minute conversation sure led to some powerful insights. Concentrate on the words your customers use. Find the ones that are repeated. Then unleash those same words back onto the marketplace.

For an HDTV

YOU: Why did you start shopping for an HDTV?

MALE CONSUMER: Well, the football season was starting and I wanted a second HDTV in the house. This one was for my den.

YOU: What were the most important features to you when you were shopping?

MALE CONSUMER: The picture, of course. It had to look great.

YOU: Does it?

MALE CONSUMER: Oh yes. Spectacular.

YOU: Spectacular how?

MALE CONSUMER: First of all, everything is incredibly sharp and bright. It's not a 3DTV, but it looks like it could be. Almost three-dimensional. Second, I was blown away by how much of the background of the picture came into focus. The audience in reality shows. The crowd in football. The rooms in television shows. It's amazing. I couldn't believe how much I was missing.

(THE AUTHOR: Boom!)

YOU: How does this TV improve your life?

MALE CONSUMER: Well, my wife and I can now watch two high-def programs at the same time. That right there was worth the $500 I spent.

YOU: What does that mean to you, watching two shows in HD at the same time?

MALE CONSUMER: Freedom. Sports. My Giants. My '49ers. My shoot-'em-up movies. Whenever I want. And I don't feel bad that I'm keeping my wife from watching her shows. She works hard, and she deserves to watch what she wants.

YOU: So this TV is just yours? You are the only one who watches it?

MALE CONSUMER: All mine!

Wrap here. You've got more than enough.

Let's review the invaluable nuggets this five-minute conversation uncovered.

- *I couldn't believe how much I was missing.* Are you kidding me? This one statement is a gold mine: *True high-definition: You won't believe how much you were missing.*
- *Freedom.* This interview uncovered a potentially powerful marketing angle for you: talking to consumers about buying their second and third HDTV. Sports. Soaps. All mine! And no guilt. Everybody watches what they want. *A second HDTV will improve your marriage!* It's somewhat tongue in cheek, but you're not exaggerating. It's not your words. It's your customers'.

For an Online Data Backup Service

Let's look at what an interview looks like for a service.

YOU: What's your favorite thing about our backup service?

SELF-EMPLOYED CONSUMER: The peace of mind. The fact that everything happens automatically.

YOU: Tell me about that. What does peace of mind mean to you?

SELF-EMPLOYED CONSUMER: It means my hard work is always safe. It means that even if my system crashes—and God knows systems crash—my documents are always protected.

YOU: Talk to me about automatic.

SELF-EMPLOYED CONSUMER: It's idiot-proof. I don't have to remember everything. It's like a savings account that you make deposits into every month, automatically, without thinking. Eventually, you realize you're rich. With this, I realize there's a collection of my work on your online drive, and it goes there automatically. It doesn't matter if I forget. You keep me safe.

(THE AUTHOR: Aha!)

YOU: Why did you pick us?

SELF-EMPLOYED CONSUMER: Well, honestly, I loved what your customers had to say. You're not the cheapest, but your testimonials were the strongest. By a lot.

YOU: What was it about our customers' statements that made you feel comfortable?

SELF-EMPLOYED CONSUMER: There were a lot of them. And they were all happy. That made me feel safe.

YOU: Safe?

SELF-EMPLOYED CONSUMER: Yeah. Not only is my data safe with you—but I'm safe. There was no risk. Your customers were happy. You guarantee your service or you'd give me back my money. I felt safe.

YOU: How do you talk about our backup service to your family and friends?

SELF-EMPLOYED CONSUMER: Well, I don't really say much, but that's because I don't ever really have to think about it.

YOU: But if you were to describe our service in a few words, what would you say?

SELF-EMPLOYED CONSUMER: Automatic peace of mind and safety.

Pretty good, right? You can go to the bank with that tagline. Also, note this person's emphasis on your happy customers. Companies in the consumer electronics industry don't focus enough on their happy customers. Don't underestimate the power of satisfied peers. Those are two pretty huge takeaways from a five-minute chat, no?

And that's the point—brief conversations with customers will generate a gold mine of marketing approaches, messages, and language.

Now, can you explain to me why you wouldn't have people at your company having these conversations daily?

The Formula

Let's say you select ten different people every two weeks to have one of these conversations each business day. That means each of them would spend fifteen minutes per day, maximum, talking to your customers. But let's double it, to be conservative, and to account for leaving messages, and connecting with people live. Together, these folks would conduct 100 total interviews in two weeks.

That's 200 interviews per month, which adds up to 2,400 interviews annually. In thirty minutes per day, per employee, for ten employees at a time.

Required Reading

There's a less active way of gathering insights about your customers. I want to emphasize that this technique is not a replacement for having live conversations but a complement to the interviewing discussed in this chapter. I'm talking about online customer reviews, which are one of the tools consumers use most when evaluating products but one of the tools manufacturers underuse when evaluating consumers.

Consumer reviews on Web sites like Amazon (the deepest collection of such reviews on the planet) and other retail sites are a gold mine of your customers' experiences. They allow consumers to check out a product through the experiences of their peers before buying it. It's one thing to hold or view a device briefly at the store, but it's another thing entirely to read how 100 people use, like, and recommend that product. These review sites allow customers to talk to each other, to tell their stories.

Remember, these reviews are not to be used as a replacement for having real interviews with your consumers. Rather, they're an always-on wealth of customer experiences and emotions. Predominantly, these are the areas you'll learn about by reading customer reviews:

- How people like your products, generally.

- How this makes them feel. (They're usually either thrilled or angry; these are still really the only two emotions that motivate people to leave a review.)
- And, in less than 25 percent of the reviews, you'll learn how people actually use your product.

That's why I say that online reviews are not a suitable substitute for talking to your customers. You can't build marketing and messaging based on how much people like your products. Remember, in your interviews, you are looking for insights about what people want from you, how people use your products, and how they think about your devices. Those are the three focus areas. Online reviews usually only address one of these points, and only infrequently. However, there's a lot of value here that's being underutilized by your company. It's a quick, searchable, indexed look at how the real world feels about your technology.

In particular, these customer reviews should be required reading for your engineers. Because your engineers are usually operating in a high-tech bubble, with few insights into what real people do with the products they create, online reviews are an easy solution. I am a firm believer that all consumer electronics engineers in America should make reading customer reviews part of their morning routine. No more than five minutes per day is necessary. If your engineers did this, they would become better engineers immediately. Through greater knowledge about which part of their work excites people most—and which part frustrates them most—they would simply make better products. Reading customer reviews regularly would pull your engineers out of their techie lab bubble and orient them toward their customers, who are mainstream consumers who don't have even 5 percent of their technical abilities or assumptions.

So, I ask again: What's stopping you from making this a daily requirement at your company?

Insights from Social Media

Some consumer electronics companies have the benefit of another kind of passive consumer insight gathering: message boards and communities. Apple has more participants in these than any other company. Sites like MacRumors are filled with hard-core Apple fans, talking mostly to each other and, sometimes, to less technical consumers looking for advice. TiVo has relatively active community boards as well. For everybody else, these communities are organized more by technology category rather than by company. For example, home theater enthusiasts congregate at various community message board sites. Photography and home movie hobbyists have community Web sites as well.

• • • • •

What types of people participate in these Internet communities?

- Consumer evangelists
- Early adopters
- Hobbyists
- Enthusiasts
- Interested parties evaluating an upcoming buying decision
- Trolls (These are pot-stirrers who get a kick out of stirring up a hornet's nest—an example is a person who goes to a Mac forum to tout his new Windows computers, or Android tablet.)

As you can see from this list, mainstream consumers do not really participate in online forums. So, although the thoughts and insights from the more technical consumers that do participate are interesting, they aren't particularly useful for structuring your marketing and messaging for the mainstream. However, there are some interesting takeaways to look for here.

• • • • •

- The mood: What's the level of satisfaction? Are people enthusiastic? Are they angry? Ambivalent?
- How does what's being said about your company compare to what's being said about other manufacturers? Who's "winning"?
- Focus on the defenders. Whether dedicated to a company or a product category, these forums are filled with people who passionately defend the brand of their choice. For example, Canon users fight for their brand over Nikon, and vice versa. TiVo customers sing their preferred provider's praises over competing DVRs. Even Windows enthusiasts defend their OS. (That's right, Microsoft has defenders out there!) Listen to what these defenders are saying. What do they rail against in particular? Where do they draw the line before speaking up? And what words do they use to defend you? This language can be effective for the mainstream.

Industry Marketing vs. Evangelist Marketing: Samsung

➤ ➤ ➤

Industry Marketing

Here's a paragraph from the product page of one of Samsung's 55-inch televisions on Amazon:

> What do you get when you combine Internet@ TV with 120Hz Clear Motion Rate technology? The Samsung LED 6500. Get the best of the Web, right on your HDTV, with downloadable and customizable widgets—and coming soon, Samsung apps. Connect to friends, share pictures, shop online and more. Samsung's 120Hz Clear Motion Rate technology delivers smooth, natural action in every scene. Samsung LED backlighting technology and advanced processing deliver a picture with an exceptionally large range of contrast and color, making images appear more lifelike. And the 6500 is as beautiful as it is functional, with a design that complements virtually any room in the house.

Evangelist Marketing

What's a widget? What's a Samsung app? Is that like an iPhone app? Why would I want to connect to friends on my TV? It's a TV! This is a case of Samsung promoting its technological advances. The problem is, I'm almost certain that the company didn't talk to its customers to find out if connecting with friends or downloading—using their TV!—was something they wanted to do. Here's how I'd say it:

> Samsung is the best-selling flat-panel TV maker for a reason: our picture is beautiful, and our TVs are beautiful in your home. People buy our TVs because they like our picture better than any other manufacturer's. They call our picture brilliant, incredible, amazing, awesome, and ridiculous. This TV also connects to the Internet, so you can watch even more great content, like Netflix.

Less tech advances, more real-world value.

Chapter Summary

- The most powerful marketing resource available to you is your customers.
- The key to powerful language and marketing is to gather detailed, qualitative insights from your consumer base.
- These are far more detailed than surveys and focus groups.
- Interviews should be conducted by phone.
- Employees and executives should do the interviewing, as talking to customers will make them more effective at their jobs.
- One conversation per day, per employee, for no more than fifteen minutes each. Fifteen minutes is plenty.
- Ask about what consumers want from you, how they use your products, and how they think about your company and your products.

- Valuable consumer insights are available on product review sites.
- Also, use social media *to listen to* (not market to) your customers.

part four

The Communications

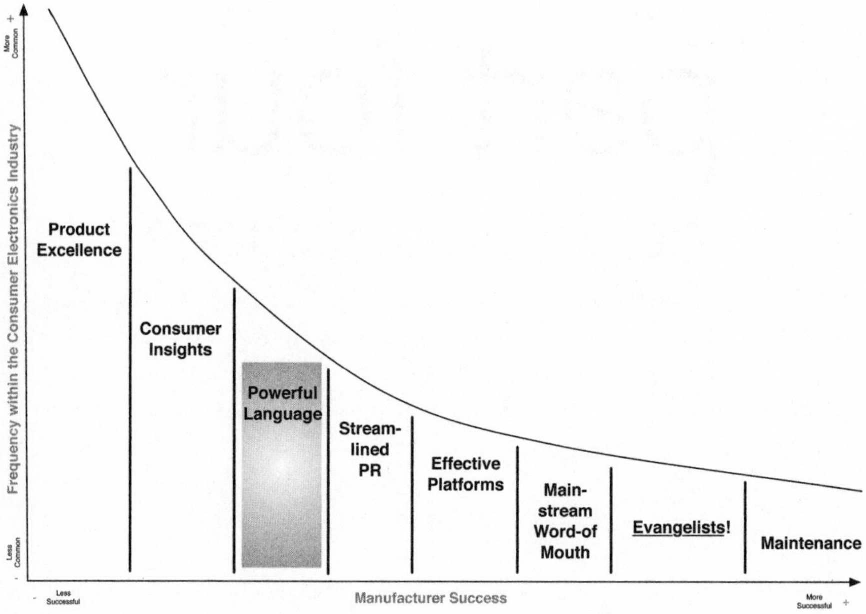

More Common +
Frequency within the Consumer Electronics Industry
Less Common -
Product Excellence
Consumer Insights
Powerful Language
Stream-lined PR
Effective Platforms
Main-stream Word-of Mouth
Evangelists!
Maintenance
- Less Successful
Manufacturer Success
More Successful +

eight

Language Is Everything

What you say about your product all but determines its success, which means that in our business, language is everything. In the previous chapter, I showed you how to uncover consumer insights. These lessons from your customers should become the foundation for what you communicate about your company and your products.

And so, in regard to getting language right, there are four key rules of thumb:

- It's all about lifestyle.
- Always tell stories.
- Always be simple.
- Always be communicating.

It's All About Lifestyle

How do you know if you're on the right track with your language? If you're talking about how your products improve people's lives, you're doing fine. Ask yourself these questions:

- How do your products make something easier, faster, or better for your customers?
- Are you helping people work? Are you helping them relax? What are you helping with? The answers make up effective marketing language.
- What part of the family unit are your products helping? Address the family, as most of your mainstream consumers have children. Many have grandchildren.

Logic makes people think, but emotion makes them act. When you talk about technical specifications, you're focusing on logic. You're telling consumers the factual, unemotional ways that your product outperforms the competition. You're trying to get people to make a buying decision by convincing them that your product stacks up favorably against the competition. This is logic. That is fine, but logic doesn't make people act. Get away from megabytes, megahertz, and megapixels. Effective language is based on talking to your customers about how your product will integrate with and improve their lives. This addresses their emotions. This makes people pull the trigger and reach for their wallets.

Industry Marketing vs. Evangelist Marketing: Canon

➤ ➤ ➤

Industry Marketing

Here's the first paragraph of a product description from Canon's product page on Amazon:

> Bring the ultimate wireless printing solution to your home or small office. The PIXMA MX870 Wireless1 Home Office All-In-One lets you print

from any room in your home and boasts incredible 9600 x 2400 maximum color dpi2 with tiny 1pl ink droplets and a 5 individual ink tank system. A built-in, fully integrated 35-sheet Auto Document Feeder means fast copying or scanning of your originals so you can tend to other tasks while the printer is at work. Its built-in Auto Duplex Printing prints 2-sided documents without having to manually flip the pages and can reduce your paper consumption by 50 percent. Combine both of those and you can automatically copy two-sided documents without having to flip any paper manually at all. Additionally, various security features like password protected PDFs let you feel safe about creating and distributing your most confidential files.

Evangelist Marketing

This is all specifications, all the time. It's even hard to get through this paragraph, isn't it? Heck, it's hard to get through the product name. It's nine words long if you include the word Canon! How many consumers do you think care about the exact maximum dpi of this printer? I'm not saying this statistic should not be communicated—it should be buried in the tech specs part of the description. It should not be featured in the second sentence of the product description! This paragraph should be using the words that Canon's customers think are important. Instead, the company is putting the words it thinks are important front and center. Here's how it should look:

The Canon PIXMA 4 [better name, no?] is a spectacular all-in-one unit that brings easy, affordable, and incredibly high-quality printing, copying, and faxing to your desk. Our customers

CONTINUED ON FOLLOWING PAGE...

CONTINUED...

> say that the quality of our prints is spectacular, dependable, and lifelike. We've designed the PIXMA 4 to print on two sides of your paper automatically, so that you use half the paper. We do everything we can to support the planet, and when you buy the PIXMA 4, that's exactly what you'll be doing, too.

It's emotional and interesting, and it uses the words of Canon customers (which I am making up here, but I've talked to enough customers for clients that I'd bet these are some of the words they'd use to describe this device).

"This Is All About Lifestyle"

❖ ❖ ❖

Chris Dobrec is senior director of product marketing at Cisco. Chris runs consumer marketing for the company's excellent Flip digital video cameras. They're affordable, tiny, and pretty much loved by anyone who uses them. Here's what he has to say about effective language:

> "The consumer electronics industry hasn't figured out that this is all about lifestyle. This is about how you impact lives in a new and meaningful way. It can't be just about a silicone wrapped piece of plastic. Lifestyle messaging is what the industry needs to evolve to."

Alex's Analysis: Your engineers can't help you figure out how to impact lives. This information must come from consumers themselves (see how to do this in the previous chapter). Also, your executive leadership must be firmly planted in this camp. Think like Steve Jobs and Jeff Bezos think.

Talk About Lifestyle

Here are some examples of how to talk about lifestyle, even for the most technical products. Of course, these lifestyle messaging points should not come from your head. Rather, they should come from your consumers, as I discussed in Chapter 7. The most effective lifestyle messaging is literally made up from the words of your customers—and you get these words by talking to your consumers one-on-one. Here are examples of wildly effective lifestyle messaging.

For hard drives

- Store up to 20,000 photographs or 30 hours of high-definition home movies.
- Automate backups by following our instructions so your memories and your work are always safe. (It doesn't matter if you include software that does this; it only matters that you teach people how to take advantage of the built-in functionality for this in Windows and Mac computers.)
- Tiny and highly portable. You won't even know this drive is on your desk. And move it from computer to computer quickly and easily.

(Note: Not one mention of megabytes or RPM. It's fine to include your capacity in your messaging, as you've trained consumers to think about your products by their storage capacities by now. But translate it into what the capacity means in their world!)

For Wireless Routers (One of the Most Technical Consumer Electronics Devices on the Market)

- The fastest speed currently available. This is all people care about. They want to know there's nothing faster. If you can also tell them it'll be fast enough for current applications for X number of months or years, even better.
- Stream video not only from the Internet but from computer to computer, computer to television, and DVR to DVR.
- Enjoy your family pictures on TV. Listen to the music on your computer through your surround sound system. Then tell people which of your other products they'll need to make this happen.

(Note: No talk of megabits per second or nanosecond, or 802.11n-or-q-or-z. These things don't mean anything to mainstream consumers.)

For Notebook Computers

- Portable not only in your house but out of it. You've got powerful computing on the deck, porch, or couch.
- Your music. Your home movies. Your pictures. These are the memories of your life, all safe, secure, and extremely portable, and all for a crazy low price.
- The LCD screen is so sharp that you can see every little detail of your children's faces. You'll never miss a detail!

(Note: I never mentioned hard drive space, RAM memory, megahertz, megabytes, or resolution. I purposely avoided a focus on work-related messaging because we're talking mainstream consumers. Don't try to be all things to all people in your language and messaging. Do try to understand exactly who you're talking to and streamline your language for them. Amazon knows exactly who it's talking to with its Kindle. So does Apple. And so does Netflix.)

Industry Marketing vs. Evangelist Marketing: Dell

➤ ➤ ➤

Industry Marketing

This is one section from Dell's Web site about its Inspiron™ 15R laptop.

Stay Connected

You're always connected anywhere you go with the Inspiron™ at your side.

Battery life

Increase your mobility with the optional 9-cell battery, with up to 7 hours and 58 minutes of battery life, or choose the standard 6-cell battery for up to 4 hours and 02 minutes of power.

Always connected

Get enhanced wireless connectivity with Dell's standard 1501 802.11g/n. Plus, you'll never lose touch with friends and family with the 1.3MP integrated Webcam and analog microphone.

CONTINUED ON FOLLOWING PAGE...

CONTINUED...

Storage

> Take advantage of a wide range of hard drive options. High-capacity hard drives up to 640GB can store up to 76 hours of Hi-def video or up to 160,000 MP3 songs.

Evangelist Marketing

Although I must compliment Dell on its impressively simple product name here, the company is blasting technical features and specifications. How will this laptop improve my life? I'm not sure. I do know I can take advantage of a wide variety of hard drive options, and connect with Dell's standard 1501 802.11g/n (seriously?). How about a bit of bite?

> Our Inspiron 15R laptop is the perfect dependable computer when a smartphone or tablet won't do. When you need a big screen, a full keyboard with actual buttons, superior battery life, and what feels like endless storage for your movies and music—all at an incredibly low price—look no further than the Dell 92 Inspiron 15R. Let the others squint at a tiny screen and type on glass without buttons. You need an actual computer, not a pretender!

This uses humor and pegs Dell's laptop to the craze in smaller, more portable devices. Why? Because when it's warranted, it's okay to go on the offense in your marketing.

Always Tell Stories

Building on your lifestyle approach, nothing in high-technology communications is more powerful than consumer stories. Stories are an extremely effective way to get across the real-life value of your products. Telling consumer stories is exponentially more effective than rattling off technical specifications. Describing real-world experiences of your customers allows new, potential consumers to imagine themselves using your technology. Customer stories build relationships with future customers because they demonstrate a strong relationship with your current customers. Specifically, I want to introduce the concept of results stories here. It's a powerful storytelling method that's extremely effective in communicating your products' value to the market.

Results Stories

Results stories are what your customers want to hear. Tell them about people just like them. They seek this information out in consumer review Web sites already. Why are you making them do extra work? Why not tell the best stories yourself? What could be more powerful than this?

Here are some characteristics of a good results story:

- It describes the experiences of a real customer.
- It details their life or work, and your product's role in either.
- Preferably, it includes a testimonial from your happy customer.
- It describes how your product has improved your customer's life. These are the "results."
- It features easily relatable life situations—you want your consumers to be easily able to envision themselves in your happy customer's situation.
- It talks about what your customer is particularly happy and excited about.

How do you obtain these stories? By asking for them. By interviewing your customers as described in Chapter 7. You simply ask them to share their results stories for you. People will be happy to do so. They'll be shocked and overwhelmed that you care enough to ask.

Once you have them, where do you use these stories? Everywhere—press releases, commercials, interviews, social media, manuals, and product packaging.

Additional Resource

• • • • •

Go to my Web site, TechnologyTailor.com, for a free video filled with examples of Results Stories for actual technologies.

The Most Powerful Kind of Language

❖ ❖ ❖

Jef Holove, CEO of Basis, former CEO of Eye-fi, on the most powerful kind of language:

> "User experiences. Period. The first impression is really powerful. If that first impression fails then there's very little we can do to make up for it. The user experience is the message. Then those people can talk about Eye-Fi. See, most companies usually start from this place of competitive

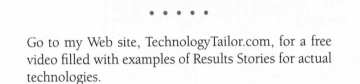

feature wars, or their place on the busy Best Buy shelf, rather than what's going to inspire people to buy this to begin with."

Alex's Analysis: Amen! Jef nailed it here; you must inspire people with stories of their peers. Talking about your customers' experiences is among the most powerful language available to you. Most manufacturers don't even get here because they're focusing on how their specifications compare to the competition's. Your specs are purely logical, which make people think. Customers' stories are emotional, which make people act. Emotion beats logic every single time.

Microsoft's Results Stories

Microsoft spent most of 2010 telling its customers' results stories in a brilliant ad campaign I discussed previously.

In its television commercials, Microsoft put the camera into its customers' living rooms. Whether these people were real customers or actors matters not. The "I'm a PC" ads communicated the ways in which Windows makes real people's lives better, easier, and more convenient. Whether it was about the convenience of watching movies all over your house or the lower prices of Windows machines as compared to the competition, these commercials featured customers telling the stories and describing their happiness. That last bit is the key.

So compare most high-tech marketing, which features you talking about your devices' technical specifications, with results stories, which feature your customers describing the life improvement your devices have brought them and the feelings that has created for them. They're happy. They're giddy even. They can't believe their good luck. Why wouldn't you want to put this front and center in your marketing?

Industry Marketing vs. Evangelist Marketing: Microsoft

➤ ➤ ➤

Industry Marketing

This is Microsoft's description of its Windows 7 Live Taskbar Previews function. It's actually a decent explanation, and relatively low on technical jargon. However, it can be improved significantly by focusing on consumer emotion.

Headline

Manage lots of open programs, documents, and browser windows easily with thumbnail and full-screen previews of open windows.

Product description

With Windows XP, a taskbar shows the programs you've got open and lists the associated files you're working with. With Windows Vista, if you hover over a program on the taskbar you can see thumbnail images of files you have open with that program. But you can't interact with the files.

Evangelist Marketing

First, this shouldn't look back at Windows XP and Vista. I understand what Microsoft is doing here: it wants to illustrate its technical advance by comparing it to previous versions. But this assumes that customers care about what happened previously, and asks them to look back, neither of which you want to do.

So, let's just focus on the relevant paragraph. It's completely functional. Step by step, Microsoft tells you where to move your mouse and click, if you were holding a mouse. Here's my rewrite:

> Windows 7 has introduced an incredible new way of seeing everything you're working on so that you can stay on top of your work, instead of your work staying on top of you. New full-screen previews directly from the task bar give you instant access to all your open programs. It's convenient, immediate, and only Microsoft Windows 7 has it.

I'm focusing on the real-world value, the human impact of the technology. Microsoft, conversely, is focusing on the technology itself.

Always Be Simple

Simplicity is missing in consumer electronics. We're far too good at overcomplicating things, so before you do anything, before you execute on any strategy, before you send another press release, ask yourself if it passes the "simple test." How does something pass the simple test? It must:

- Be brief, not verbose.
- Describe lifestyle value, not technical specification.

- Use adjectives and emotion words rather than technology jargon.
- Allow consumers easily to imagine themselves using your product.
- Be clear immediately; if the intended audience must think or work to connect your pieces, it's not simple enough... go back to the drawing board.

In the business world, Occam's Razor is interpreted to mean that the simplest explanation is the best one. Follow Occam's Razor. Focus ruthlessly on simplicity, and your language—along with your entire marketing effort—will improve immediately.

"Keep It Simple"

Steve Swasey, vice president of communications, Netflix, on one of the biggest keys to Netflix's success:

> "Keep it simple. Most folks want a product that turns on or off. Remember the flashing 12 on VCRs. I have a [cable] box and I work at a technology company in Silicon Valley, and this box has a DVR, and I don't care. I don't want it. I just want the cable. But they give me the DVR. Keep it simple. Consumers aren't stupid. We don't have time to digest that which isn't easy to digest. We spend an inordinate amount of time figuring out how to deliver our message simply. We don't use jargon. We don't use tech speak. Across the board, in our advertising, our direct mail, and our executive appearances, we keep it as simple as possible."

Alex's Analysis: As a Netflix vice president, Steve knows something about keeping viewing options simple. And as one of the three companies with consumer evangelists, the language Netflix uses couldn't be simpler: Join Netflix. Watch DVDs. Watch instantly. Note that they do not emphasize the word *stream*. That's a technical term. Rather, they use the simpler, more immediate, more emotional phrase *watch instantly*. And Netflix isn't going on instinct in making that selection; they talked to a lot of consumers about the best possible way to describe their service before implementing this language.

ABC: Always Be Communicating

You must always maintain a flow of information toward consumers. I know this is the language chapter of the book—it's here because I want to address the quantity and continuity of your language. The spigot must always stay in the "on" position. There is no upside to pausing communication. Pauses are damaging. And stoppages are deadly.

Once upon a time, Palm had evangelists—not just for the handheld devices but for the Treo smartphones as well. People loved Palm, swore by it. Back then, Palm enjoyed countless consumer evangelists. This is the company that invented the consumer smartphone! The Treo was the original mainstream smartphone—ages before the iPhone. The first Treo hit the market in April 2002, a full five years before the first iPhone. A sixty-month head start in the consumer electronics industry is like sixty years everywhere else. (The first Blackberry device came out in 1999, but it didn't have access to the cellular network back then, and was only aimed at the business market.)

But then, sometime around 2007, after the iPhone became a sensation, Palm stopped talking to people. Marketing became lethargic, and communication all but ceased. The company was still making excellent Treo smartphones, but consumers were moving on in droves, and Palm was doing little in the way of communication to stop them. Forward progress screeched to a halt.

Then, in 2009, Palm made one of its biggest product launches of the decade, the Palm Pre—a brand-new smartphone with an all-new Web-based operating system. It was a sensational product—the first truly excellent Palm device in years. And the company tried to restart its outgoing communication. There were commercials. There was a lot of media outreach. There was energy and investment and education but, sadly, there was little consumer audience for this. Because Palm was starting all this outreach from scratch, with no momentum, no foundation, nothing to build on. Over the years, Palm consumers had moved on to companies that were talking to them and enticing them. The Palm Pre never generated the kind of sales the company needed to survive, and it was eventually bought, for pennies on the dollar as compared to its peak value, by HP.

The fatal sequence began not when Palm stopped innovating but when it stopped energizing and exciting its consumers. Consumer attention shifted to companies that fought harder and more aggressively for it than Palm did. When you stop talking to consumers, you will lose them. Maybe forever.

Chapter Summary

- Focus your marketing language relentlessly on lifestyle. How do your products help consumers? How do they improve people's lives, homes, and activities?
- Instead of technical specifications, tell consumer results stories.

- Focus on simplicity because it's missing in our business. Simplify your message. Simplify your language. Streamline. Shorten.
- Never stop communicating with customers because that is your momentum. If you stop, it is nearly impossible to restart.

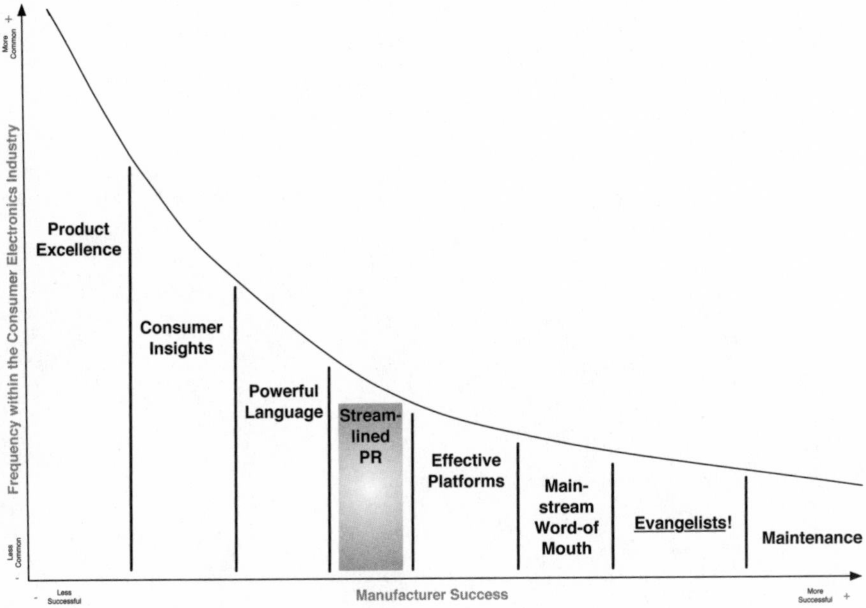
Frequency within the Consumer Electronics Industry
More Common +
Less Common -
Product Excellence
Consumer Insights
Powerful Language
Stream-lined PR
Effective Platforms
Main-stream Word-of Mouth
Evangelists!
Maintenance
Manufacturer Success
- Less Successful
More Successful +

nine

How Your Public Relations Kills Consumer Electronics

Your public relations campaigns are killing you.

I say this without a shred of doubt. I am more certain of this than anything else in this book. Your PR department is incorrectly positioned within your corporate structure, and at the same time, your unsophisticated public relations associates are making too many needless mistakes. They pitch too much, too generally, rarely tailoring anything to any particular recipient. Your media relations people aren't relating; they're blasting mediocre, often awful, press releases to people who write for a living! Meanwhile, your executives and leadership are not nearly involved enough with the media. All together, this is a mind-blowing recipe for failure, and that's exactly what results: the media hates your press releases and usually doesn't even read them (I know, I've been there—most tech writers HATE press releases); your media relations people get turned down or ignored 99.9 percent of the time; as a result, they burn out quickly (which is why most media relations people are young, inexperienced, and annoying to journalists); your products, each the result of millions, sometimes tens of millions of dollars of research and development, hit a wall at launch, which is supposed to be the most exciting time in a product lifecycle.

Additional Resource

• • • • •

I've created a special set of multimedia additional resources and education for consumer electronics public relations professionals on my Web site, TechnologyTailor.com. There is no cost. Just click on the picture of this book on my Web site to access it.

So many products die at the hands of your PR professionals that you might as well build a special graveyard. The epitaphs would read: *Here lies yet another device, once so full of promise, turned to dust before its time by horrific public relations.*

If you are reading this, and you have anything to do with making, marketing, or selling consumer electronics, these problems affect you. The PR disaster that I'm detailing here affects the vast majority of technology makers and *nearly every single public relations agency in the business*. Perhaps the most stunning fact in all of this is that it is entirely avoidable.

You don't *have* to write terrible releases.

You don't *have* to blast hundreds of journalists with them.

Your PR people don't *have* to function as glorified paper shufflers, mindlessly pushing press releases and follow-up inquiries.

And yet, it happens daily, hundreds of times, all over our industry. This is such a huge, expensive, and unnecessary problem that I am going to spend two chapters on it. In this chapter, I'm going to dig deeply into detailing the problems. In the next chapter, we'll dive just as deeply into the solutions. I will tell you exactly what you are doing wrong, and then I will lay out exactly what you should do to make it right. Follow my advice and you're certain to increase sales. Ignore it, and you are simply accepting the current dysfunctional state of (public) affairs. These problems are costing you millions. Fix them.

Imagine Being a Journalist

Imagine being a journalist covering technology or, God forbid, a tech blogger.

Every day, you interview, write, submit, then rinse and repeat.

Deadlines loom, editors breathe down your neck. Readers criticize mercilessly (ever read the comments on your local newspaper's Web site?).

You do all this with no job security. If you're a newspaper person, most of your colleagues are gone, either retiring early or making their way as freelance writers. If you're a blogger, you are in the business of producing words and Web pages. If you get paid at all, it's laughably little. If you work at a large blog, you can be replaced by a college student. (I mean no offense; it's just an incredibly difficult way to make a living.)

When you finally submit a story you've carefully shaped and molded throughout the day, there is no feedback. No compliments. (Newspapers are notorious for this: the only time you ever hear anything from your editor is when he has a problem with your work. If the story is excellent, you hear nothing at all.) What is your reward? Beginning the next story. The next deadline.

On top of all this, all day, every day, you receive press releases that suffer from all of the problems described above—they're bad-boring-poorly-written-confusing-annoying. You get a hundred more of them daily. And they're all blasted. Every single one goes to a large group of people—hundreds? thousands?—just like you. You know immediately that, like you, there are countless others considering writing about this very topic right now. So much for scooping the competition.

You're tired. You're worried about your job. And you get myriad horrible, blasted, anonymous pitches daily. Guess what you do with these pitches? Speaking from experience, I can tell you that you do one of two things: glance at them for five seconds each before being 100 percent certain that these pitches are so not for you, or simply delete them on the spot.

The solutions to this sad and widely accepted phenomenon are simple. I repeat: it doesn't have to be this way. By your actions, you actively choose for it to be so. Today, for most of you reading this, your public relations function is working against you, and that's putting it mildly.

Public Relations Problems and Solutions

In Chapters 7 and 8, we covered the concepts that effective marketing begins with consumers and that the most successful public relations language comes from the words of your customers. Everything should start with consumers. The fact that it does not is problem number one. But we've already covered that, so let's look at the various specific problems with today's high-tech public relations function.

Problem #1: PR Is Too Far Removed from the Action.

One of the fundamental issues in technology PR is in the corporate structure. At most companies, the public relations department is too far from the part of the company where strategy is formulated. The problem is that information flows one way, from engineers to product managers to marketers, and finally to public relations (see the diagram in Chapter 1). PR is the last stop for your messaging before it leaves the company for the media and the public. The problem is that by the time your messaging reaches PR, it has already been shaped, molded, and more or less finalized. Your PR team's task is simply to distribute the finished message. They have little to do with formulating the message. They're rarely involved with the strategic work of developing messages that will resonate with consumers.

Ironically, tragically, of all the departments at your company involved with structuring marketing and messaging, the PR department is the one that's closest to consumers. It is the door through which your consumer communication leaves the company. Your media relations folks are also among the first to get feedback from those receiving your messages—the media. If they have any experience at all, they have a good sense of the kind of approach and message that would generate a positive response with the media. And yet, all they do is blast what's been formulated without them.

Solution #1: Involve PR in Strategy Creation

Solving this problem—like most of the problems this book addresses—is pretty easy: get your PR department involved much earlier in your strategic processes. They know what works. They are the department that's the closest to consumers. Why wouldn't you want to tap that knowledge and integrate it into your messaging development? They know what the media thinks (even if all they know is that the media is not responding to their pitches). They know what resonates with consumers and media outlets. Involve them in the early stages. In fact, it wouldn't be a bad idea to make a direct trade in your marketing strategy development meetings: swap out your engineers and swap in several public relations people.

Problem #2: PR Professionals Don't Have a Grasp of the Company's Strategic Direction.

Because your PR folks are at the end of the communications line at your firm, many miles from where strategy takes shape, they have little grasp of your strategic direction. They don't know why you're doing what you're doing. So when journalists ask relatively simple questions (like *What are your goals with this product?*), the media relations person pitching to them often does not know the answer. In the PR–media relationship, there is a lot of *I don't know, I'll get back to you* going on. This puts the brakes on the process of getting coverage on a product, and is one of the many annoyances the media faces.

Remember, these are the staffers you're putting in front of people who will determine your products' future. Don't you think they should be armed with the **why** as well as the *what* when speaking with the press? Don't you think you should put them in the best position to succeed before they are to deal with the media?

Solution #2: Educate Your PR Team About the Why, *Not Just the* What

Your public relations teams usually have your talking points down pat. They're terrific at reciting them. Sometimes, it's the only thing they do very well. But they lack any insight about your strategy because you don't share it with them. Why not? Because management likely views PR staff like the media does: unsophisticated and not entirely relevant. But that doesn't change the fact that they're still between you and the press—and, frankly, between you and success. Don't send them into battle unarmed. Teach them about why things are being done. That way, they'll be able to answer more of the media's questions without slowing down the publicity process.

Problem #3: Press Releases Fail.

Let's look specifically at press releases, which as I've said throughout this book, are pretty much terrible. There's no question that your press releases hurt you more than they help you.

Here are eight reasons most press releases fail:

1. They're ill-conceived. The focus, as is the rule in consumer electronics, tends to be on high technology instead of high value. Most press releases focus on obscure technical details instead of consumer results stories. Instead of capturing the media's attention, most press releases confuse and frustrate the media.
2. The writing is bad, which means that most releases read like they were a chore to write (which is exactly how release writing is perceived within the PR department).

Your releases are difficult to get through. If a journalist can't get through the first couple of paragraphs of your release, do you think you're going to get coverage?

3. They're usually filled with grammatical errors. Remember who the audience is: professional writers and editors—people who "do" grammar for a living. For goodness sake, put your press releases through a couple rounds of edits.
4. They're not interesting. On second thought, they're not only not interesting, they're actually boring. Your goal is to fascinate, excite, and stoke the imagination of the journalist. You want them to say "Wow." You want them to think of an interesting way to write about or present your product to their audience early in your press release. If you don't think your press release can make a journalist say, *This would be cool*, then don't send it.
5. They rarely tell a good story. They almost never talk about real people who have used your products. They never help a journalist see the story he or she would tell about your product or service. You're making your recipients work too hard. Try starting every press release you send—every single one—with a story about a real person whose life your product has improved. This would force four great developments: you'd actually have to speak with your customers, your press releases would instantly become more interesting, you'd help journalists immediately see the value of your products, and you would get more coverage. Do you see any downside here? Worried about repetition? This sort of repetition would be welcomed by the media. Because the kind of repetition you're blasting out there now is hurting you, frustrating journalists, and costing your company millions.
6. They're often impossible to understand. I wish I could share with you some of the press releases I've received

in the last week alone. I want to, but I've always said that it's never my business to hurt the companies or the people in this business. Everything I've done in my consulting practice is focused on helping manufacturers. I will abide by that principle here, but I will say this: sometimes, not only do I not know what your press release is trying to say, I don't even know what the product is! Here's a good rule of thumb: never send a press release that contains an acronym. They're damaging. And annoying. Here's another rule of thumb: don't assume that journalists receiving your press releases know anything about what you're talking about. Remember, journalists are in the business of making your products and services interesting and easy to understand for their audience. Help them. Don't work against them.

7. The product's value isn't clear. You're not explaining how your product or service will improve people's lives. You're too focused on the technology. I know some of these points overlap, but I don't care. Don't like the repetition? Imagine receiving over a hundred bad press releases every day. Over and over. People learn in different ways, and I'm trying to get across my points from as many different directions as possible. Perhaps one of them will stick with you. Perhaps the sheer repetition will wear you down. Your press releases rarely tell journalists what's good about your product in a way that's interesting to them. Think about that!
8. They fail to capture the recipient's attention. Your subject lines are awful. They're usually longer than what fits in the subject field in the journalist's inbox. Don't ever copy and paste your press release's headline or first sentence into the subject line. That's lazy. And incredibly harmful.

Speaking of lazy, your press releases are blasted anonymously to hundreds or thousands of journalists at a time. There is no sign of a relationship with any particular journalists in your blasted pitch emails. You may not realize it, but here's what you're saying to recipients: you are one of countless people considering covering this right now; I don't want to make an effort to position this to you personally, and to your audience; and I don't care that you know that I don't care.

Industry Marketing vs. Evangelist Marketing: Motorola

➤ ➤ ➤

Industry Marketing

Here is the first half of the press release Motorola used to announce its XOOM tablet:

> Motorola Mobility Brings Motorola XOOM™ Wi-Fi to United States
>
> March 16, 2011
>
> LIBERTYVILLE, Ill. – March 16, 2011 – Motorola Mobility, Inc. (NYSE: MMI), today announced the upcoming availability of Motorola XOOM™ Wi-Fi edition from leading retailers across the United States starting March 27. Amazon.com, Best Buy, Costco, RadioShack, Sam's Club (select locations), Staples and Wal-Mart will be offering the 10.1-inch widescreen HD tablet with Android™ 3.0 (Honeycomb) through both online and retail store channels. The MSRP for Motorola XOOM Wi-Fi with 32 GB of memory will be $599.

CONTINUED ON FOLLOWING PAGE . . .

CONTINUED...

"Motorola XOOM is a truly innovative tablet—its design, coupled with being the first tablet to have Android 3.0, results in a user experience that is one-of-a-kind," said Dan Papalia, vice president of retail sales for Motorola Mobility. "We are now continuing to expand the choices available to consumers with the Motorola XOOM Wi-Fi to be available soon from numerous leading retailers in the United States."

In addition, the Motorola XOOM Wi-Fi will be available to commercial IT channels and regional retailers through a distribution agreement with Synnex Corporation, and regional carriers through Brightpoint, Inc.

Motorola XOOM showcases the innovations of the Honeycomb user experience—including widgets, true multitasking, browsing, notifications and customization—on a 10.1-inch widescreen HD display, enabling video content that's richer and clearer than ever before. With a 1GHz dual-core processor and 1 GB of RAM, Motorola XOOM delivers exceptionally fast web-browsing performance. The latest Google Mobile services include Google Maps 5.0™ with 3D interaction and access to more than 3 million Google eBooks and apps from Android Market™. Motorola XOOM also supports a Beta of Adobe® Flash® Player 10.2 downloadable from Android Market, enabling the delivery of rich Flash based web content including videos, casual games and rich Internet applications.

Evangelist Marketing

This is an availability press release. Its purpose is to tell the media that the Motorola XOOM Wi-Fi model is now available at retail. It does that relatively well in the first paragraph. Everything else is a disaster. The executive quote doesn't add value, and feels forced and repetitive. The commercial IT channels sentence is useless because it has nothing to do with the consumer retail outlets this release focuses on. It's almost like it was added just in case some IT press happened to be accidentally included in the blast. And the last paragraph here is a horror. Go ahead; try to read it in its entirety.

Here's my take on the last paragraph:

> The Motorola XOOM is the most advanced Android tablet you can buy. It is the only tablet to feature the latest Android operating system—which is easy, powerful, graceful, and a pleasure to use. At least that's what our customers tell us. The XOOM lets you watch movies, listen to music, and view photos—not to mention bringing you a full, brilliant, touchscreen Internet connection. The XOOM is basically limitless because you can expand it in countless ways with downloadable apps from the Android Marketplace. Oh, and you know how the competition doesn't let you see online video that's in Flash? We do! That means the XOOM brings you full access to video sites like Hulu and others.

Again, the focus is lifestyle, emotion, and the real-life outcomes.

Sample Press Release Headlines

If you are not yet convinced that press releases in their current form are a bad idea, here are some headlines that I received in a recent twenty-four-hour period. The headlines are more than enough to make my point. I won't put you through the pain of reading the body of these releases. Some ground rules: these press releases are public information because they were distributed to the media and in many cases posted on each company's Web site. Still, I am taking steps to protect the guilty here by removing any references to company names or details that can give away the exact product or the maker. Here are the headlines, straight copy-and-pastes from my email:

> *Company XYZ Expands its Line of Noise Cancelling Headphones, While Introducing Innovative NoiseSomethingSomething /digital Technology*
>
> ***Analysis:*** Why are you blasting this to countless journalists? It's a product introduction of headphones, which have been on the market for some years. You introduced digital Technology (capital T)?? This line was in the headline of the press release and the subject line of the email, which is just another lazy, annoying thing PR people to do to journalists. If a member of the media can't read the entire subject line on his screen, what are the chances he's going to end up covering your new product?
>
> *Company XYZ Showcases Innovative Android Embedded Software Solutions for Consumer Electronics, Automotive and Mobile Industries at CES 2011*
>
> ***Analysis:*** So what? Why did you send this to me and hundreds of others? What about this can be even possibly remotely interesting? I bet you weren't even interested when you wrote it. Now, if you told me how your new embedded software would change people's lives, I might open your

email. "Company XYZ revolutionizes auto maintenance for millions of consumers."

Company XYZ Becomes First Consumer Electronics Manufacturer to Launch Cloud-Based Interactive Television Solution With ActiveVideo

Analysis: If I read this headline four times, I might possibly begin to grasp what it means. Maybe. Here's how I'd say it instead: "Company XYZ Changes Television Forever." That is interesting. It makes me wonder, "How?" and, "Why?"

COMPANY XYZ IS FIRST TO LAUNCH NEW LINE OF PORTABLE TELEVISION PRODUCTS FOR EASY RECEPTION OF BOTH STANDARD AND MOBILE DIGITAL TV BROADCASTS

Analysis: This came in ALL CAPS, just like that. This headline tries to squeeze two paragraphs of information into a single line. I have no idea what a mobile digital TV broadcast is. If that was added to create interest, it does the opposite; it adds confusion.

Overall, I know none of the people who sent me these press releases. I can't recall meeting any of them. A big reason for this is that some of the announcements did not even come from named people. They came from companies—your PR agencies! How you can allow your agency to send releases this bad with these terrible headlines without so much as a name in the "from" field of the email is beyond me. How is this allowed to happen? These are multimillion-dollar products they are killing!

Press Releases Are for *What*?

• • • • •

There's a man in the PR industry who runs a widely known public relations service. He told me recently that everybody knows that press releases are not for getting coverage; rather, they are for improved positioning on search engines once they are posted to your Web site. What? This incredible statement is one of the craziest things I've ever heard. Why send press releases to journalists at all if they're just for increasing the ranking of your Web site? Why do manufacturers spend tens of millions on media outreach and courtship annually? I'm not going to spend any additional time debunking this ridiculous theory, but I wanted to present it here because the PR industry is filled with crazy assumptions—like this one, and the one about social media PR actually being useful to anybody (it's pretty much useless—more on this in Chapter 11).

Make no mistake, press releases are not for search engine optimization or any other crazy thing besides this one desired result of obtaining coverage for your company and products in the mainstream media. That's it. Your goal is to alert consumers through the media they frequently turn to for information. If you are in PR, your one goal in the world should be for major media—TV, radio, and newspapers—to catch what you are pitching.

Solution #3: Stop Sending Press Releases and Send Personal Communications Only

If you agree with me that these press releases are not only unhelpful but usually harmful to your public relations effort, then how about entertaining the idea of eliminating them entirely? If the media hates them, and you don't particularly enjoy writing them, and the release itself, as discussed in detail in the previous section, is not very good, what if you cut them out entirely?

If you stopped sending press releases tomorrow—if your PR effort quit relying on the net negative known as the press release, here's what would happen:

- You would be forced to build relationships with journalists instead of blasting them with impersonal, unhelpful press releases.
- You would be forced to learn what the journalists you deal with actually cover. You would have to understand their interests.
- You would be forced to gather insights on each journalist's audience. Who reads? Who watches? Who listens? What's the demographic of these consumers? Do they work? Do they have families? What are their interests? How do they spend their time?
- You would actually need to customize your pitches for each audience. You'd focus on areas that are interesting to the people who actually consume the news each journalist creates. That's right: this means each pitch would be different.

And as a result, you would communicate far more with journalists personally—by phone and by email—as you present your story. That's because you won't be blasting releases, you'll be building relationships. You'll be helping each media member tell an interesting story. You'll be talking instead of pitching. Journalists will find you valuable. Trust me, it's easy to stand out among the people that the media hears from daily.

But how can we eliminate press releases? I can hear you asking. *That's what our companies and clients pay us to do!*

Precisely. They're putting their multimillion-dollar products into your hands, and you are preemptively turning your single best opportunity for coverage with a journalist into near-certain failure by mass mailing bad, boring press releases. Let me say it differently—and I know I'm repeating myself from the beginning of this chapter, but this is game-changing critical: you are killing good consumer electronics with bad press releases.

Guess Which Company Doesn't Send Press Releases?

For those of you fundamentally against eliminating press releases, do you know which company doesn't send press releases at all? As a matter of fact, this company doesn't really talk to the press at all, as if by rule. I'll give you a hint: it happens to be the single greatest marketing company in any business. Apple does not talk to the media except at carefully scripted and choreographed events that are keynoted by CEO Steve Jobs. By not talking to the media, Apple encourages the media to talk about it. See more about this in Chapter 12.

"What Apple Does Is Tease"

"It's like a really beautiful girl with just some clothes on. All of these other companies want to go expose themselves. What Apple does is tease. It's all about a tease. The more you tell a kid I'm not going to let you have that cookie, the more they want the cookie. It's a superbly run tease."

—John Sculley, former CEO of Apple

Alex's Analysis: This was John's answer in response to my question about why he thinks Apple doesn't talk to the press today. It's true, isn't it? If you give a child an entire package of cookies, and then another, and another, eventually he will lose interest. Health problems aside, those cookies get old and boring. Then, on top of it, you keep endlessly telling the child about all of the wonderful ingredients inside the cookies—precise measurements of wheat flour, sugar, ammonium bicarbonate, and beta-carotene (That one is for color, my boy). Here's a question: Does he care about the ingredients (technical specifications, in our world)? Of course not. Plus, he has been exposed to the cookies nonstop. He has lost interest. He's over them. You've ruined this brand of cookies for him.

Problem #4: Media Relations People Are Too Young and Unsophisticated.

Media relations work is difficult. It's mostly anonymous because these folks are pitching en masse and have met few, if any, of the people to whom they are sending press releases. It involves a lot of rejection, as nine-and-a-half out of ten terrible pitches are turned down (and I'd estimate eight out of ten are not read beyond the first sentence or two). Because of the preponderance of negative outcomes, the burn-out rate is very high for most media relations people. People move on—to other jobs, and other careers—early and often.

Because of all this, media relations people tend to be young and unsophisticated. They're usually in their twenties, and in one of their very first jobs. They have little experience, yet they're being asked to deal with highly educated, sophisticated, and extremely cynical journalists. They come at journalists with just the talking points you arm them with, and have a difficult time discussing anything else.

Why would you want these people essentially determining the success or failure of your multimillion-dollar product research and development investments? Because that's the position you are putting them in. They don't deserve to be in this position. It's not fair to them, and it's not a comfortable place for them, which is obviously confirmed by the results they (don't) generate. Further, and more importantly, it's not fair to you, your executive leadership, and everyone else working toward the success of what you create. This is not the media relations people's fault. They don't put themselves in position to fail. Management does.

So ... stop it! Put them in a position to succeed. Help them. If you don't, if you do nothing, they'll continue killing you.

Of course, there are exceptions to this rule, but they are exactly that: rare exceptions. Because of these problems, good media relations people are held in high esteem by the press. They are personal, personable, helpful, and fast. There are so few of them that they are literally almost worshiped by the press. I know that when I was writing my *Chicago Tribune* column, I would seriously consider everything that one of these nearly extinct excellent PR professionals would send. In fact, I almost felt obligated to help them by doing a piece just because they were so good at their jobs and so helpful to me. And, actually, I wrote many pieces only because one of these people made the pitch. They all turned out well because the PR person was so good, sometimes even thinking through the story with me. That's a mutual respect and trust that is nearly impossible for young adults just out of college to attain. They are training on the job and, because of the circumstances, many of them never get out of the training stage.

Problem 4B: The Media Does Not Enjoy Being Managed

One of the big problems in consumer electronics public relations occurs widely, causes lots of damage, but is universally accepted as simply the way the system works. It's not questioned. It's not challenged.

And it continues happening just because that's the way it has always been done.

I'm talking about the fact that PR people feel the need to manage the relationship between the media and your executives. They like to "own" media relationships. That sets up this scenario: a sophisticated, cynical journalist and a high-level, highly compensated company executive must run around the rules of a PR associate armed with little more than a few talking points. It's ludicrous! Here's how it looks:

- The media cannot talk to the executive without the approval and involvement of the PR associate.
- The PR person is often connected to the actual interviews by conference call.
- They add either nothing or very little to the conversation, often breaking up any rhythm that has been established.
- These PR people are viewed as an unnecessary barrier between media and your executives.

Journalists hate this system. They hate being "managed" and "owned." And don't kid yourself: executives are not fond of having to be managed by people their children's age. This is not a good system. It's a damaging one. And yet it occurs every day.

(As an aside, I realize I'm not gaining any fans among the PR community here, but please keep reading. I am not suggesting that your company push you aside and do the work of media relations without you. I'm actually saying exactly the opposite: you can quite easily create powerful results for consumer electronics companies. What is required is a shift in thinking and a slight adjustment in how you go about your work. It'll make a dramatic difference in how media relations is executed and lead to powerful results.)

Solution 4A and 4B: Let Your Executives Manage Media Relationships

There's a simple solution to both problems, but your instinct will probably be to dismiss it immediately: What if your executives strategically managed media relationships directly?

It's a radical idea, and most people immediately default to, "But that's not the way we do it." Right. Except this is a better way. Stay with me on this one.

The media is tired of dealing with unhelpful media relations people and their press releases. Meanwhile, your media people are tired of the regular rejection, and it affects their performance. Neither the press nor your company's executives enjoy being managed by young PR people. The system is broken. But if you allow your executives to develop relationships with the media directly, imagine how stunned journalists would be if your leadership called or emailed them directly. Imagine the publicity you'd generate if journalists were connected directly to the leadership of the companies they cover.

"But they don't have the time."

Of course they do. And if you're an executive reading this, then of course you do! It only takes five minutes per day. Here's the model: assign twenty members of the media each to, say, ten executives. Contact one per working day. Phone or email, it doesn't matter. In a month, you get through the entire list. Next month, you start again. Put your media people on your calendar, one per day. It only takes one contact per day. You can do it in your car or at the airport. Then, if they want to work on a piece about what you pitch, hand it off to your PR team to handle scheduling. If you're an executive, you're already doing interviews, so this would be nothing new. The only extra commitment this adds to your life is five minutes per day, with twenty key media people. Spread this tiny task across ten executives—and your company leadership is now making 200 press contacts per month, and 2,400 per year. My guess is that it results in hundreds—as in 200 or 400 or more—of press pieces.

Why do it this way? There is no shortage of significant advantages.

- Your leadership will build relationships with the media instead of your PR people, who simply blast pitches to the press.
- Your executives will be able to communicate in ways your young media relations people cannot.
- Your executives have insights into corporate strategy, which your PR department cannot reference because they do not know it.
- The press will be thrilled to hear from somebody other than twenty-three-year-olds.
- Your publicity results will skyrocket.
- You'll establish an effective core of media relationships to leverage. Don't be misled by your PR agency; you do not have these relationships today. At least, not any level that's beyond that of a mass-mailer-to-annoyed-journalist relationship.
- You will have a huge leg up on the competition, which is almost certainly not going about its PR in this manner. It's not difficult to stand out in the crowd that the media deals with. I know. I've been there.
- Relieved and grateful media contacts are the most effective kind, and that is what you are creating here. You are bringing them value instead of pitches, ideas instead of press releases, relationships instead of blasted emails.

Here's how the communications flow and responsibilities would break down:

FIGURE 9.1
The Ideal Media Communications Flow

YOUR EXECUTIVES	YOUR MEDIA RELATIONS PROFESSIONALS
1. Pitch one media member per day, by phone or email.	
	2. Manage the list of who is dealing with whom, and track the communications.
3. If there is interest in coverage, connect the media member with your PR team.	
	4. Distribute additional information if the media is interested.
	5. Manage the process of working on stories with the media.
6. Do the interviews.	

As you can see, there is only one extra step for your leadership, and it only lasts five minutes per day. Your media people are still intimately involved in the publicity process. The press is happy. And you will get far more coverage than ever before.

There is no downside here.

Chapter Summary

- Poor public relations is harming very good technology products.
- The changes to implement are not difficult to execute, but they're a challenge because they go against the way "you do things."
- Journalists are routinely overwhelmed with mass-mailed, poorly written, uninteresting press releases that are not based on any sort of relationship between your public relations department and the journalist.
- Your public relations team should be more involved with the strategic orientation of your marketing.
- Consider eliminating press releases altogether.
- Allow your executives to manage a small number of media relationships personally, with your media relations team managing the logistics.

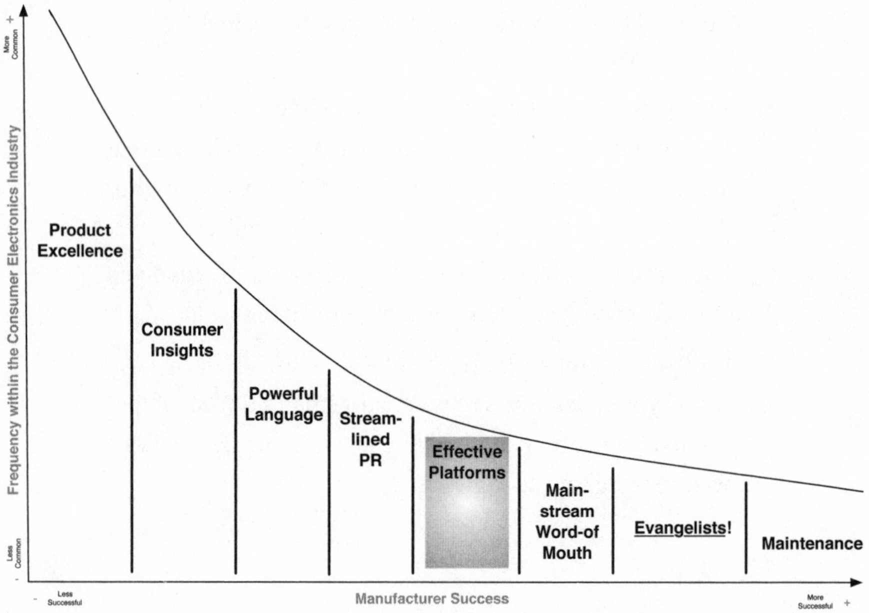

Frequency within the Consumer Electronics Industry
More Common +
Less Common -
Product Excellence
Consumer Insights
Powerful Language
Stream-lined PR
Effective Platforms
Main-stream Word-of Mouth
Evangelists!
Maintenance
Manufacturer Success
- Less Successful
More Successful +

ten

Your Communications Platforms

Once you've perfected your language and streamlined your public relations, it's time to start delivering your carefully honed messages back to customers. Remember, you're basically repackaging what your customers have told you, and aiming it right back at prospective customers. An important step toward attaining evangelist consumers is to talk to your customers from the right places. I cover these platforms in this chapter—beginning with my take on the recent sprint toward social media. The rest of this chapter addresses how to leverage (and not leverage) the blogosphere, big media, your product packaging, and one of the biggest missed marketing opportunities in the entire industry, your product manuals.

The Downside of Social Media

There has been a huge marketing push into social media over the last several years. Especially in the consumer electronics industry, manufacturers have rushed to Facebook and Twitter to "engage" with their customers. Words with little real-world value have become buzzwords in consumer tech marketing; *engaging the customer* and *joining the conversation* have been elevated to the same level as *revenue* and *investors*. Truly, social media is the new focus of the marketing world. A slew of new agencies have opened touting their ability to help you leverage social media in marketing. Marketing and public relations agencies that were actually effective at producing results in the real world have shifted their entire operations toward Facebook and Twitter. Social media has become all the rage in our industry.

So allow me, if you would, to rage against social media for a moment. And please remember that this is a book about marketing consumer electronics. I'm not coming at social media from a personal brand perspective, where it can be quite valuable. It's also useful to new companies and start-ups, in initially spreading awareness. The danger here is that you're attracting early adopters, who, as we've discussed, are often an obstacle to acquiring mainstream consumers.

As for the manufacturers pouring people and effort into Facebook and Twitter, I'm sorry, but social media is not the place to invest millions of dollars to market to mainstream consumers. You won't reach Mom and Dad on Twitter. And while you may find them on Facebook, do you think they're going to buy your HDTV or smartphone because you have a Facebook fan page? Or because you're paying for Facebook text ads on the right side of the page?

Here's the thing: Facebook is mostly used by consumers to connect informally and loosely with distant family and acquaintances they'd rather not call or email. People are just as likely to be receptive to your marketing messages as they are to the farm animal their annoying "friend" needs. Facebook serves its purpose as a loose online social club. As for the consumer-corporation relationship on Facebook, September 2011 report by consulting firm Bain & Company found that the average Facebook users will "like" no more than seven comrpanies or brands. That's it. Just seven. And my experience has been that even if they do "like" your brand, they're mostly looking for discounts and deals. Are you willing to risk millions of dollars in the effort to be one of the seven?

Twitter, conversely, is strictly a business-to-business marketing vehicle. But good luck actually getting your tweets read by more than a few people. Even if you're "only" following 500 people, there's little chance you'll be physically able to read all of their tweets. Most Twitter users follow thousands of people. In fact, it's an unwritten code of conduct that you should follow those who have followed you. So what you tweet may actually be read by 5 to 10 percent of your followers, and that's being generous. On top of this, Twitter is filled predominantly with people looking for business. Don't believe me? Spend five minutes trying to count how many "social media experts" or people who "help you find your true calling in life" you see in the main Twitter stream. I wonder how many of them are in their parents' basements.

Further, consider this research from a study released in March 2011 by Yahoo and Cornell University: Twitter has more than 200 million members. However, the researchers found that 50 percent of all tweets are sent by just 20,000 people. Put another way, *0.05 percent of Twitter members are responsible for half of everything transmitted there!* Worse, most of the messages sent by these "Twitter elite" are re-tweets of others' information. This is where you want to try to market your products and your company? Why?

Why do you think people will buy your devices if you talk about them on Facebook or Twitter?

They won't and they don't.

"You Can't Create Heat Through Social Media"

"Here's my point about social media: the hotter your product is, the more social media can amplify that heat. But you can't create heat through social media. You can't make your offer hot by tweeting. Social media is not intended to be an advertising medium. It can have marketing

CONTINUED ON FOLLOWING PAGE...

CONTINUED...

consequences, but those are unintentional. Social media is good for customer support. Other users are a better source of customer support than the company itself."

—GEOFFREY MOORE, consultant and author, *Crossing The Chasm*

Alex's Analysis: This is a nice rule of thumb: if you have a successful product, consumers will use social media to fan the flames. If you have a product that's relatively unknown, social media won't help you make it known to the mainstream. You might get a few retweets among the Twitterati, but those are exceedingly fleeting and aren't worth much. The key is knowing that you can't control when your customers will use social media to talk about your product. It's up to them, and there's little you can do to influence their behavior directly on social media. That's why there's little reason to include social media in your marketing to mainstream consumers. If it happens, it's a nice surprise. But don't plan on it.

On the other side of this continuum, there are some reasonable uses of social media.

Effective Social Media Implementation

Of course, there are some valuable uses of social media.

- *Customer service.* Assign one or a handful of customer service specialists to assuage frayed feelings via social media. Twitter is excellent for this. Search for various keywords related to your products and your company, and respond to concerns. Do so publicly as opposed to in a private message, and demonstrate how addressing customers' concerns is a critical part of your company's mission. Dell and Comcast are two companies in our industry that have done this with great results. Zappos, the Internet shoe and attire retailer, built its entire reputation by doing this. It increases goodwill and generates word-of-mouth marketing. If you want to really blow away the masses, involve your high-level executive. Have a different executive respond directly to one customer concern per day.

- *Listening.* What are people saying about your company? What are they happy about? What are they complaining about? How are they using your products or services? What do they say about the value of your goods or services? How does your device improve their lives? You can gleam some powerful marketing language from carefully observing what people are saying about you on Twitter, and to a lesser extent, on Facebook.
- *Promotions and Discounts:* Facebook has developed into an excellent medium to convey periodic promotions and specials to your customers. For example, offering a Facebook-only coupon or limited-time discount works to build your repute among your most loyal followers. Basically, when you do this, you are rewarding people for being fans and followers.
- *Contests:* Same benefits as above: building goodwill and good feelings.

There has been another lamentable corporate development with the recent rush to social media: corporate executives who try to raise their own profile via social media who are actually hurting their company in the process. They could be talking to your actual customers instead of tweeting about what flight they're about to take. I'd love to know why these people think it's interesting, helpful, or valuable for anyone to hear about where they're about to fly to. Who cares? People don't care about where you're eating lunch either.

But it makes us more accessible; people like that.

No. People like good products that improve their lives. You should be spending your available time either making them or figuring out how to talk effectively to people about them.

I even know a former high-level consumer electronics executive who amassed a lot of Twitter followers and left his job to become a social media expert! As an executive, he was one of a select few, but as a Twitter marketing expert, he decided to become one of the millions. By the way, while he was becoming a social media star, the company whose marketing he helped run did not perform well at all. There is little direct correlation between social media success and real-world business success. Social media is fleeting. Consumer electronics buying decisions are carefully considered. Social media is fast, short, and immediate. Consumer electronics buying decisions require people to commit their hard-earned money. Attention deficit disorder is at the core of the social media experience (one reason, perhaps, for its meteoric rise among its most loyal fans). Tweets and updates are brief and are on the screen for only seconds before being pushed out by newer versions. Experts have found that a Facebook update is only on your followers' wall for less than an hour.

Also, recently, many companies have started encouraging people to interact with their social media specialists on their Facebook discussion boards. Be *very* careful with this. As you can imagine, many of the comments, sometimes *most* of them, are negative. People communicate more often when they're angry than when they're satisfied. There are now famous brands on Facebooks with hundreds of pages of angry comments from their customers. Is this the image you want to project? Is this a risk you want to invest millions of dollars in? Remember, the social media experts dealing with the complaints are much like public relations specialists: young and at low levels. Many times, their only response is to communicate that they have forwarded the complaints to their customer service departments. If you take a step back and analyze this objectively, I think you'll agree with me that this sort of "customer engagement" is not helpful to anybody involved.

Another study released in the Fall of 2011 by Gallup found, after talking to 17,000 U.S. adults about how they use social media found their results "debunked three big myths about social media," one of which was "that it effectively drives customer acquisition." It does not. Rather it engages your existing customers. And that's a fine use of Facebook, as I outline below. Help your existing customers on Facebook. Support them. Do this effectively, and, as the Gallup study found, "you'll encourage them to engage *their* social networks on your behalf." (Emphasis added.)

Finally, consider what my friend Chad Barr, an accomplished Internet strategist, has to say about social media: "Companies have not figured out how to use social media most effectively." I agree with this wholeheartedly. I think that over time social media will become more useful and productive in consumer electronics marketing. But it shouldn't be your responsibility to figure out how to make it so. This will be a collective effort, and the final answer is still years away. Until then, moderate your use of social media. Participate, but remember that it should be a relatively small piece of your overall marketing strategy. And, remember that when you invest in social media, you're taking resources away from other kinds of media that actually will produce results.

What kind of media? Bigger media.

The Blogosphere

Blogs that cover consumer electronics reach approximately as many mainstream consumers as Twitter (not many!). There are two handfuls of blogs that reach the mainstream—and these are blogs in name only; they have more in common with major news organizations than blogs. Historically, of course, blogs started out as one person's thoughts on a simple diary-like Web page. Well, blogs have come of age, and now the *Huffington Post* is a mainstream (if left-leaning) news site that also covers technology. It's good to be there. Conversely, blogs that cover technology specifically—like *Gizmodo* and *Engadget*—are mostly frequented by highly technical types who have a deep understanding of electronics. The majority of these folks would fall into my early adopter category.

Here's a look at the top ten blogs on the Internet, according to *Technorati* at the time of this writing, and their typical audience makeup:

- The *Huffington Post*—the most popular blog on the Internet according to *Technorati*. Attracts mainstream consumers. A fine target for your communication.
- Six of the top ten blogs—*TechCrunch*, *Engadget*, *Mashable*, *Gizmodo*, *Boing Boing*, and *ReadWriteWeb*—are considered tech blogs. It's okay to be there—but understand that you're reaching the people who have an interest in this type of material. It's not Mom, Dad, Grandma, and Grandpa you'll be talking to here. (Of course, some will be mothers and fathers, but they'll be of the highly technical variety.)
- Rounding out the top ten are a gossip site (*TMZ*), a media news site (*Mediaite*), and *Gawker*, which falls somewhere between gossip, news, and media.

So, where do you want to be to reach typical consumers? The *Huffington Post* and maybe *Gawker*. That's it.

I'm not suggesting you avoid blogs. If you get inquiries from them, treat them promptly and professionally. But don't go out of your way to get coverage in the blogosphere because it won't help you reach the most valuable audience you have.

If you insist on pitching to blogs, here's a quick idea: Remember all those young and inexperienced PR media relations folks that used to send out press releases to mainstream media? Ask them to focus on the blogosphere. The process of pitching and following up is very much the same. But while your executives are managing the big media relationships (see Chapter 9), your PR folks can dig into the blogosphere. There's not as much to gain, but there's also much less to lose. Just a thought.

Big Media

If you want to reach mainstream consumers, the single best place you can be is big media: newspapers, magazines, television, and radio. It's true that the Internet has had a huge impact on major media, but guess which one the mainstream flocks to when it comes to making consumer electronics buying decisions? Not social media. Not blogs. They're not there. Rather, they're reading newspapers and magazines, watching TV, and listening to the radio. Yes, still.

Simply stated, if you're not leveraging big media to tout the value of your products, you're not reaching mainstream consumers.

From highest to lowest in terms of value and results, here's a list of media placements, starting with the most desirable:

1. Editorial reviews and demonstrations in the best-known outlets.

    - Newspapers: The *New York Times*, the *Wall Street Journal*, *USA Today*. These are three with the biggest impact.
    - National talk shows: *Oprah* used to head this list. Today, it's *Ellen DeGeneres*, *Rachel Ray*, and *Martha Stewart*. Getting on their list of "favorite things" is proven to produce a wave of new customers.
    - National television shows: These are fleeting. After your two or three minutes, the video gets buried somewhere on their Web site for a relatively short amount of time. The print publications have comparatively more lasting value. They lay around all day physically, and then they're archived online for years—maybe forever.
    - National radio programs: There's a fairly long list of nationally syndicated radio shows that talk about technology regularly. These shows

reach millions, and you want to be here when it comes to radio.

- Local television and radio programs: There are well over a thousand TV and radio programs that air locally, from the biggest market in the United States to the smallest. They need good content daily (and they rarely have it). Help them, and get yourself some very valuable publicity in the process.
- Paid broadcast endorsements: If you can have an expert endorse you on the air, even if you pay for it, and your relationship is disclosed to the station and the audience, the endorsement can be very valuable for building awareness of your product among mainstream consumers. Media tours are one of the highest value broadcast media activities you can engage in, and the key is to use a known, trusted endorser. Your own spokesperson doesn't carry nearly as much value.

2. Magazine reviews, in order of value:

   - Nontechnical magazines with big readership are best: publications that cover news, fashion, parenting, and travel is where you want to be.
   - Technology magazines are the blogs of the offline world. They don't have a big mainstream consumer audience, and, therefore, are not where you want to be.

3. Advertising and Commercials: Ironically, the place where companies spend the most money is the least valuable in terms of ROI. People gloss over commercials. They fast-forward past them on their DVR, and flip right by them in print publications. Investing in

commercials is incredibly expensive, and is rarely worth your while.

4. Also, of course, big media Web sites are a desirable target for your messages and for editorial coverage. This means that I consider sites like CNN.com, MSNBC.com, and FoxNews.com big media. NYTimes.com, WSJ.com, and USAToday.com, too. Here's the key: nearly all Web sites of big offline media properties also include a large amount of content that appears only online. Entire sections, as well as columnists, can be Web-only versions. Often, these pieces have bigger audiences than anything in the print versions of these publications. Educate yourself about the writers and editors that handle this. Their audience is as mainstream as the offline media's. You want to be here.
5. Big media is the one place we know consumers go regularly, and both the media and its audiences love talking about technology. If you're leveraging the opportunities above, you'd be well served to think about how to expand what you're doing. If you're not here, why not? And how soon can you be here?

Product Packaging

In Chapter 4, I talked about packaging as an opportunity to make a powerful first impression. If your product box is boring and highly technical, consumers will gloss right over it. If your box is bright, simple, inviting, and creates good feelings for consumers, it will literally build their anticipation for the product. It's an advanced look at the good feelings that await them inside the box.

In this section, I want to look at the product package as a communications platform, not just for your customers but for the big-box sales associates who could use all the help they can get. Often, a customer's buying decision comes down to the information they read on your box. Whether at the electronics store or the office supply store, the details on your box influence thousands of people across the world every day. How much attention do you give it?

Packaging Today

The majority of product packages today aren't taking advantage of an opportunity to teach, market, impress, motivate, and/or enthuse customers. Take printers. There's always a big picture of the printer, and some product specifications. The package will typically list the various sizes of prints the unit can create, as well as resolution of the print, the paper tray capacity, connectivity options, etc. The boxes often feature various highly technical logos, symbolizing different wired and wireless communications technologies the printer supports. The box will tell you about the color LCD screen, the memory card slots supported, and the print speeds. So, you'd see facts and figures like these on a printer box:

20 ppm black, 15 ppm color

Scanning resolution up to 1200 dpi optical, maximum size 8.5" x 11"

Paper handling, 4" x 6" to 8.5" x 14"

SD, CF

60-sheet input tray, 25 sheet output tray

What does this do for you? Does it excite you about this printer? Does it motivate you to go with this brand over another?

The same thing happens with nearly all packaging, so I can safely assume that your packaging, like your marketing and communications, is focused on your technical specifications and not the real-world, specific ways that your devices can improve your customers' lives. The boxes, in their current presentation, do little besides communicate unemotional tech specs.

What Packaging Can Be

If you want to know how to use packaging to tantalize potential customers, walk into an Apple store and look at their walls filled with product boxes, from floor to ceiling, looking sleek, sexy, interesting, and magnetic. Here are some traits of Apple's packaging:

- The product rules. On all of Apple's boxes, the product is front and center, either visible through a see-through plastic box (in the case of iPods) or taking up the entire front of the box.
- And it's only the product, and, possibly, the name of the device. That's it.
- Specifications are difficult to find. Sometimes they're on the back of Apple's boxes. Sometimes a few differentiating, identifying facts are listed next to the small bar code on the back of the box.

The purpose of Apple's boxes is to mesmerize the prospective customer with the product's design. *Here is what our device looks like. Imagine yourself using it. Wouldn't it feel good to own one of these? This is why we're the best.*

But what if your product isn't as beautifully designed as Apple's? Why not feature a photo of a person—or a group—using your device and looking very happy and satisfied. This way, we can see your product, but more importantly, we can see how happy it makes people. Or include testimonials from customers. If I can read about what real people love about your product, I'll be far more inclined to buy it. Why not feature positive reviews from media, especially if they're from recognizable sources? Take a page from Hollywood studios—they put positive endorsements front and center when promoting a film. Lead with other people's positive impressions.

Also, show me the product being used in its natural environment, where the value it's adding is clear. For example, going back to printers, show me your printer in a modern, elegant-looking home office, printing out something interesting. Or surrounded by framed photographs and a happy family enjoying and taking the images in. If you're packaging a digital camera, show me a family event—a barbecue, a child's birthday, a family vacation, with the camera in the middle of the action. If it's a smartphone, show me someone connecting with his loved ones while he's away from home. If it's an HDTV, show me a family watching sports together. If it's a computer, which is more boring than all the rest, show me how it keeps real people connected in an interesting way. If it's something even more technical and emotionally bland like a hard drive or memory card, show me how it can store the photos and home videos that are the memories of my life. Literally, show me home movies and photos on the box of your hard drive or memory. Then tell me how many of each (typically) it can hold.

Ironically, words don't help much on packaging. They crowd out the device. They fire information at the prospective customer. They confuse because, when there are words, they tend to be too technical. Obviously, you need to list some technical specs on your package. Here's a rule of thumb: everything you need to detail can be done using one-quarter of the back panel of the box. If you don't think this is possible, look at Apple's packaging. The rest of the space? Use it to draw people in. Help people imagine how wonderful it would feel to own your products.

Product Manuals

I bought a digital SLR camera recently and was surprised to find that the manual that came in the box was rather thin—just sixty-nine pages cover to cover. It seemed to touch on most of the basics, but it was very light on the details. So I did a Google search for my camera model and "user manual" and was surprised to find that it was more than three times the length of the one included in the box. The online version, which, to the manufacturer's credit, was available for download as a PDF from the company's Web site, was a whopping 207 pages. It included far more features and covered topics in far greater depth than the paper manual.

What gives?

Why didn't they include the good one with my product? Were they trying to save money on paper? What if I wasn't technically savvy enough to track down the useful manual? Perhaps it was on the CD that came with my camera, but I didn't even check. I learned everything I needed to know when I tracked down the digital manual, with three times the information of the one that came in the box.

Earlier in the book, I mentioned that an audio/video receiver that I bought came with such a terrible user guide that a customer had taken it upon himself to create an online guide that was actually helpful. The Web site is called "XYZ-to-English Dictionary" where XYZ is the name of the manufacturer. The first section of the manual is titled "Setting up your receiver, in plain English."

How many tech products have you purchased in the last five years that didn't even have a manual? Instead, the company provided the Web address where you can go to download the user manual. Because when it comes to helping customers get the most out of consumer electronics, our industry is clueless. The onus is on the customer to figure out how to use the product they've purchased, with little to no help from the manufacturer.

Why does this happen? How can this be allowed to happen?

I have an idea, a working hypothesis: I don't think there's anyone at most consumer electronics manufacturers who has the talent, the resources, or the mandate to write a good, helpful, easy-to-understand manual for the buying public. Think about the people at your company—am I wrong? I bet much of your internal systems documentation is more interesting, helpful, and easier to understand than the manuals you put into your products' boxes. The problem is that it takes a unique set of skills to put together a good manual: you need to understand the product fully (an engineering person is probably best for this), and you need to be able to make your guide easy to understand (there is nobody worse than an engineering person for this). It's sad that all the public would be thrilled with a booklet that teaches how to use the product in an understandable way, and nothing more. The bar is so low. And I can't think of a single manual that I read in the last five years that meets that criterion.

But what if we got radical and actually aimed for interesting in addition to understandable? What if your manual actually talked about how your product can improve the customer's life? Instead of simply describing the function of the buttons or the features, what if you described real use cases? So, while telling your functionality story, perhaps you can intersperse real-life use scenarios: at home, at work, on the road, when watching sports, when viewing a movie, while photographing your kids on the beach, while driving.

Customer Stories

Better yet, what if your manuals told the stories of real customers? Case studies. A handful per manual. Sure, it's a new product, and it may be hard to find people to profile, but here are a couple of options: profile a few beta testers, describe the lifestyle improvement the product delivered to an employee who got to use the product for a month before release, or simply tell the stories of customers of the most recent product previous to the current device. These profiles don't need to be long. Each customer's story can simply focus on how he or she takes advantage of one feature in your product.

If you don't have anyone at your company who can describe your product's functioning, interview customers, and write about all of it in interesting, compelling ways, you should bring them in on a contract basis. If you haven't heard yet, a lot of good writers are available for hire, and they're used to working as freelancers. They'd be happy for the work. And it wouldn't cost much at all. For a onetime $5,000 investment (that's a ballpark number, and your figure may well be significantly less), you'd create a wildly valuable return. You'd literally be making news. Journalists would fall all over themselves to cover your product manual that includes customer stories. The day your first manual hits shelves, you'd immediately gain a huge advantage on the competition. And most importantly, you'd build loyalty and customer energy, which is exactly what this book is about. A tremendous product manual would go a long way toward helping you develop consumer evangelists.

By the way, you are not looking for a technical writer to make an effective product manual here. You're looking for a magazine or newspaper writer. A journalist would be good. Look for people who know how to ask good questions and mold what they're told so that it's helpful to readers. You want somebody who can explain technical concepts in understandable ways—but even more critically, you want someone who makes it interesting.

The Perfect Manual

In a perfect world, if you could do anything you wanted—and you can—here's what a perfect product manual would look like:

- It would be written in a conversational, understandable way, in English from the beginning (instead of translated, roughly, from Korean or Chinese).
- The manual's structure would be oriented around how real people use it—starting with the common uses of the device or service, following with deeper and deeper functions.
- Each section would include a quote, in a box, from a real customer. "I can't believe how great my pictures look with HDR photography. And the camera does it for me. I just turn on the bracketing feature, and it takes three pictures, at varying exposures, which I later combine in Photomatix on my Mac." (And then a note for where the customers can find more Photomatix information in your manual.) Just like that, in simple English, easy-to-understand words, and yes, referencing outside complementary products within your manual. If they can help people get the most out of your product and brand, why not tell them about it?
- Periodically, there would be two-to-three-page-long case studies on real customers. A photo of them, if they allow it, would be helpful. This would thrill and shock

consumers: a real person, who is very much like them, taking advantage of this feature or that. These case studies would include details on how the person uses your product or service and how it improves his or her life. Go heavy on quotes. Let your customers talk to your customers in your product manual.

- Every manual should have a section on frequently asked questions but written conversationally instead of technically. Make the questions about real-world use scenarios and problem-solving for real people. That means that you cannot talk to your engineers at all while structuring the FAQ section.

The perfect manual is not difficult to write; just detail the instructions in an understandable way and infuse, surround, and enhance them with real people's stories, thoughts, and examples.

And if you don't want to waste the paper needed to print a long manual, include the manual in the box on a CD that's clearly labeled, that has nothing on it but the manual. Emphasize your product manual. The point is to communicate that teaching and helping your customers is a priority for you.

Missed Marketing Opportunities

From a business perspective, you're missing a huge marketing opportunity by not including an effective product manual with your product or service. (If you're a consumer-facing service or Web site, you'd be well served to push a good manual to your customers by email. Don't ask them to come find it on your Web site, buried somewhere in the Support page; email it to them. Put it in their hands.)

In fact, you should start thinking about your manual as a first-impression marketing tool. This is, of course, a critical time to market, because this is when customers are forming their opinions. They're evaluating. They might even still return your device if it's not what they expected. Help your customers to get the most out of your devices by teaching them—and showing them that you care about them getting the most out of your devices.

It's inexcusable, really, that most major consumer technologies have commercial guidebooks that teach consumers far more effectively than the product manual. What's happening there is that the author is marketing herself and her brand on your back. Further, and more damaging, the consumer is turning to another resource to learn to get the most out of your tool. You are losing control of your own post-purchase marketing at that point. By including the same unhelpful manual, you remove yourself as an influence, creating a vacuum that's filled by someone else. Also, you know those "Missing Manuals" and big, fat guidebooks that fill the computer and photography sections of a bookstore? That's an industry valued in the tens of millions of dollars that's built in the vacuum you created. Why would you voluntarily give up a huge opportunity to help market to your new customers? (They are arguably the very best kind of customer—you've already sold them—now all you have to do is make them happy!) Some clients answer this question by telling me, "It's just the way it is now; our manuals are bad." You write them, so fix it!

Chapter Summary

Once you develop and hone your language and public relations effort, it's time to talk directly to consumers. Here are my dos and don'ts:

- Don't expect social media to connect you to consumers.
- Rather, use Facebook and Twitter to address any customer problems you come across, and as a place to listen. What do people say about your company? Your products? It's valuable as a monitoring tool.
- Blogs are of limited value with mainstream consumers. They mostly reach early adopters, and you have many different paths to these kinds of customer. Plus, as we discussed in Chapter 6, focusing on early adopters actually prevents you from reaching the mainstream.

- Do work aggressively to spread your message in the major print and broadcast media.
- You're missing a big opportunity with the current state of your product packaging. Use it to allow consumers to imagine themselves using your device when they're making a buying decision.
- Your product manual must be improved dramatically. Create something that is straightforward and easy to understand; it's also critical to profile actual customers in it. You may have to hire a freelance journalist for this. A technical writer doesn't have the skill set needed, and most of you probably don't have anyone in house who does. (If you did, your manuals would be much better already.)

part five

Consumer Evangelism

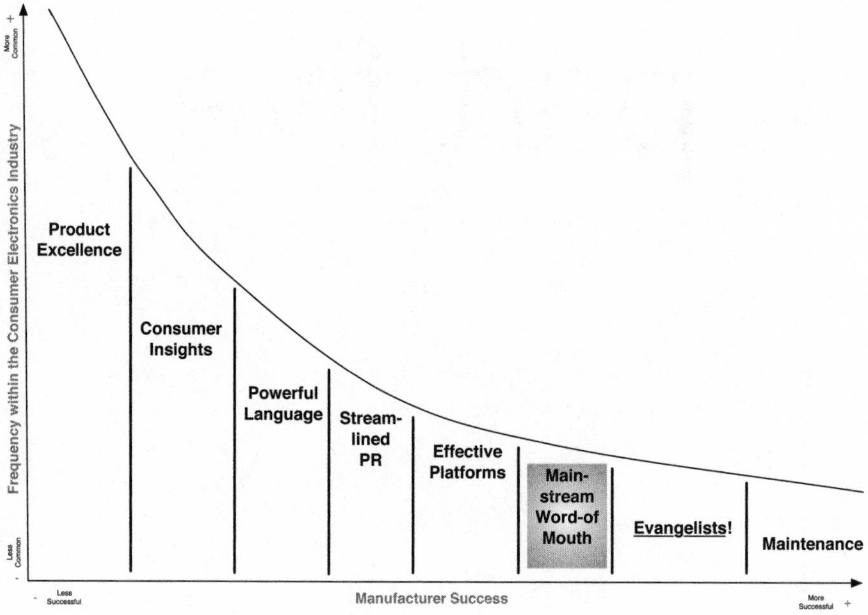

Frequency within the Consumer Electronics Industry
More Common +
- Less Common
Product Excellence
Consumer Insights
Powerful Language
Stream-lined PR
Effective Platforms
Main-stream Word-of Mouth
Evangelists!
Maintenance
- Less Successful
Manufacturer Success
More Successful +

eleven

Word of Mouth and Buzz Building

If you take the steps described in this book—from perfecting your product to understanding your customers and how they think, from streamlining your public relations to talking to consumers from the right platforms—if you execute these improvements pretty much in order, there is little doubt that you will succeed in getting consumers to talk about you.

In this chapter, I want to analyze the company that happens to be the very best in the world at creating consumer buzz. I want to look at what they do to create this constant awareness, and the communities that they leverage to do so.

You don't have to re-create the wheel on this. The wheel already exists—let's study it.

How Apple Builds Buzz

Apple builds and fuels its word-of-mouth machine in two steps, so first, I'll address what Apple does that's absolutely unique to them in the industry. Then I'll address the kinds of people who fuel their word-of-mouth buzz.

Here's what Apple does to create, catalyze, and nurture the intense mainstream interest in its communities:

- *Best-in-class products*—Apple products are not just great, they're accepted by the majority of mainstream consumers as simply being the best of their class. Ask most people who have used a Mac, and they'll tell you that based on functionality and user experience alone, there is no better computer than a Mac. The same goes for the iPod, iPhone, and certainly the iPad. There's no better app store than Apple's, and iTunes is the very best online music and video store on the planet. Although I believe these statements to be true, it's mainstream consumers who are making them. Also, note how few products Apple actually makes. They do computers and less than a handful of accessories, some iPods, a couple of iPhone options, and less than a handful of iPads. And some software. That's it. That's the core, and Apple aggressively says no to other product ideas and opportunities. They don't do video games. They don't do cameras. They don't do televisions or refrigerators or PDAs or security systems. This is what trips up some of Apple's major competition in the market. I'm talking about companies like Sony, Microsoft, and HP. Home in, and then hone your product. Perfect one or two products. Becoming best in class in a single category will be more powerful to your ability to create word-of-mouth buzz among consumers (not to mention your top and bottom lines) than making above-average products in twenty categories.
- *Industry-leading design and user experience*—This builds off of having best-in-class devices. Their design is good, and the resulting user experience is so exceptional that

Apple surpasses every other company in consumer electronics in the good feelings it creates for its customers. I talked about the Feel Good Factor in Chapter 4. Nobody creates better feelings, and stronger positive emotions, for its customers than Apple.

- *Tantalizing events*—Here's all you need to know about this: when Apple merely reserves event space, there is an uproar in the technology media and the blogosphere. *Oh my gosh, Apple is finally announcing it! Could it be a new iPhone? Will it have seven cameras, like I hoped and dreamed? I can't wait until that keynote! What can it be?* Like kids in a candy store, Apple observers salivate at the thought of a big announcement from their home-team tech maker. Remember, technology is like sports, and Apple fans are of the die-hard variety (Chapter 1). The rumor machine churns year-round for Apple, and their events, which only happen once or twice each year, position the rumors on the front pages of major newspapers around the country. One other point here: Who announces products for Apple? Either the CEO or another high-ranking executive of the company. It's done personally. It's done emotionally—find a Steve Jobs product announcement on YouTube and you'll see the kind of emotional language he uses with every single product announcement. How do other companies announce their products? With a press release blasted to thousands of journalists, right? It's not only impersonal, but it's downright annoying to the media. That means that you're actively frustrating the media on your product's first day! See the difference between Apple and all the others?
- *Not communicating with the press*—As I detailed in Chapter 9, no other company avoids talking to the press like Apple does. Of course, this goes against the accepted protocol in consumer electronics. Apple allows the

rumors to build by not denying them but also by not commenting on them. There is a system to how Apple does this, and not talking to the media is a central part of the process. I sometimes wonder what Apple's sizable PR team does. I know they write press releases, but the announcements are only made on the day of the product launches, which usually happens at an Apple event. Nothing is announced before the event occurs. But the rumors are buzzed about constantly. There is not a day in the year when Apple rumors are not flying around. Think about that! There's even an active message board called MacRumors with thousands of Apple enthusiasts sharing tips, ideas, and speculation. Enthusiasts flock to these communities because there is such great interest in the company, and so little official information coming from it. People have asked me if I think Apple might plant the rumors itself. I have no inside information on this, but I would not be surprised if this is the case.

- *Carefully manage the drip, drip, drip of information*—Book the facility. Drip. Newspapers report on it. Drip. Your CEO responds to a customer's email. And it immediately gets posted on hundreds of blogs and message boards. Drip again. Columnists guess what's coming next. Drip. Consumers read the columnists, and tell their spouses about what might be coming. Drip. Spouse researches it online, and then hits the message boards. Drip. It's on the radio. It's on TV. It's everywhere. Before long, the drips become a downpour of consumer buzz and word-of-mouth messaging, all of which the company merely manages with little active contribution. Rather, it's the wizard of consumer buzz hidden behind the curtain, pushing buttons, managing mouthpieces, booking facilities, preparing emotional keynote product unveilings, watching lines wind around the block when a hyped product is launched (at least once a year), watching products fly off the shelf, watching revenues skyrocket, profits, too, and enjoying stock prices that double, again and again.

"Are People Having a Joyful Experience with Our Product?"

❖ ❖ ❖

"Apple really only builds for one consumer, and that's Steve [Jobs]. He's the Buddha consumer. He has this incredible consumer experience vision. He's their identity. Then he beats the crap out of everybody to get to his vision. It's not fun to be anywhere near him, and I say that only with the deepest respect. Any other maker will ask, *What are our price margins? What are our volumes? What technology platform are we on? Can't we improve our supply chain? Can't we get a better shelf placement in Best Buy?* It's everything except what Jobs is asking, which is, *Are people having a joyful experience with our product?*"

—Geoffrey Moore, consultant and author, *Crossing the Chasm*

Alex's Analysis: Several of the executives and leaders I spoke with for this book mentioned Steve Jobs by name. They were always the ones to bring him up, not me. He was the only executive to be mentioned by name. That's just a small sign of just how closely even his peers look to what he does and how he does it. I think every consumer electronics executive should have it as a job requirement to spend a few hours per month studying the methods and approaches of Steve Jobs.

Apple's Communities

Now that we've seen the *how,* let's look at the *who*. This is what Apple's communities look like, and how they feed each other with energy and curiosity—this is Apple's Community Ecosystem:

FIGURE 11.1

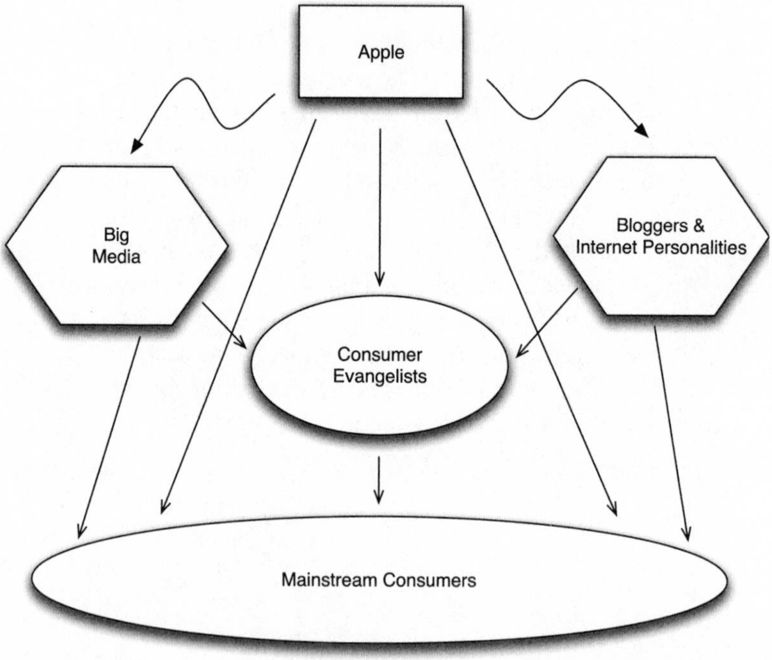

As you can see, for our purposes, Apple directly and indirectly manages four groups of people. Also, it's important to point that high-tech early adopters are nowhere in this ecosystem. In fact, for Apple (and for Netflix and Amazon's Kindle), consumer evangelists have replaced early adopters. This is an infinitely valuable swap to make, and I'll detail the traits of consumer evangelists in detail in the next chapter. For now, let's analyze each of these communities.

- *Big media:* The press loves everything that Apple does. Every. Little. Thing. It even loves things that Apple doesn't do. Major newspapers, in print and online, will run articles weekly or more frequently about what might be coming from Apple. Think of that! What other company enjoys this kind of unsolicited attention from the media? Manufacturers would kill for this sort of attention. Here's the thing about the major press: the vast majority of journalists—whether in print or broadcast—are Mac users. So immediately, Apple has a huge advantage on the competition, and just as importantly, every other company is at a major disadvantage. The media isn't using Microsoft Windows, so how can Microsoft ever be on an even footing? The good feelings that journalists get from their laptops are created in Apple's labs, not Microsoft's. Or Sony's. Or HP's. This may seem like a nuance, but it's quite a big deal. Walk into the pressroom of any consumer electronics-related trade show and you'll see hundreds of working press people, bloggers, and analysts, the vast majority of whom are writing their stories on some version of the MacBook. Do you think they're influenced by the technology with which they spend their entire day? The simple act of deciding which product they buy affects their perception of the market. When they bought their personal laptop, they chose Apple. Apple won. It's their preference. Do not underestimate the significance of being personally adopted by the media. Put it on your list of marketing priorities.
- *Bloggers and Internet personalities:* There are literally thousands of bloggers who do nothing but cover Apple news and products. Does IBM have thousands of bloggers covering it? Does Samsung? Does Google even? Nobody has created a more passionate set of influencers than Apple—and they did it by using the techniques

I described in the last section. Interestingly, for most consumer electronics companies, blogosphere buzz follows product announcements in the form of reviews, reactions, and analysis. For Apple, blog buzz turns into the news! Big media literally reports on the rumors the blogs analyze. And that's the thing—hundreds of blogosphere reactions are posted every single day about what Apple might do! Analyses of Apple rumors—likes, dislikes, etc.—occur daily.

- *Consumer evangelists:* Guess who follows the big media's reporting and the blogosphere's rumor-crunching with rapt attention? Apple's legion of consumer evangelists. These are people who seriously consider buying every single Apple product just because Apple makes it. This is the very best kind of customer. It's easy to have early-adopter evangelists. But when parent and grandparent consumers sing your praises and spread your gospel as truth, you stand alone. Well, you stand with Apple.
- *Mainstream consumers:* This is the 95 percent of the market that are not early adopters. These are the regular tech shoppers who are not yet evangelists, although they probably know some. And they're certainly consuming the major media, and many of them follow technology news online. These people couldn't get away from Apple news if they tried. Because it's everywhere, right? And aside from official news sources, they're hearing the news from their friends and family—their fellow consumers. They are referred to Apple on a regular basis. And it's not *go buy this* either. It's *listen to how wonderful this is!* Nothing is more powerful in our business than genuine enthusiasm for and belief in a product.

Authenticity

❖ ❖ ❖

"I think when you see an Apple ad, regardless of how outrageous it is, it is an absolutely authentic conversation. Guys and girls dancing on a billboard on a silhouette; [the wildly successful marketing phrase] Think Different: Absolutely authentic. Very few people can do that because it's Steve Jobs and Apple. When you see someone else attempting that, customers say, *You're not Apple*. So immediately you're not authentic. Other companies trying to copy Apple is not authentic.

"Marketing has to be authentic—if it's authentic, I'll engage. I'll remember it. Selling is fine. Marketing is fine, but only if you're trying to do it in a very authentic fashion."

—Tony Lee, vice president of marketing, TiVo

Alex's Analysis: I love this concept of authentic marketing. When is marketing authentic? When it focuses on your consumers' experiences and lives. When it focuses on how your product improves their lives. When you discuss your value in an easy-to-understand way. When you connect with people. When you use words that you know will resonate with consumers and you know they'll resonate because it was consumers who gave you that language in the first place.

CONTINUED ON FOLLOWING PAGE...

CONTINUED...

When you have consumer evangelists, your marketing is automatically authentic. What a luxury! It's authentic because you've been wildly successful. You have the public's trust. You make great products. And you talk to people about them in emotional ways. Most of all, your marketing is authentic because it's evangelists who spread your message to other consumers. Nice, right? Not only is your marketing automatically perceived as authentic, but it's also executed for you, for free, by passionate customers who will do a far more effective job than you ever could. There is no downside to having evangelists.

Word-of-Mouth Buzz Is What Tips You

The buzz we're discussing in this chapter is what tips you from being a company with enthusiasts to a company with mainstream evangelists. The key is that the word-of-mouth buzz must occur among mainstream consumers. Early adopter buzz isn't helpful to us. Blogosphere buzz is usually fleeting—they have to create copy. Unless you have evangelists like the three companies I've identified in this book, you're usually just helping bloggers reach their daily word count.

That said, the blogosphere is an important tool to use in generating excitement among your target audience. So is the big media. And so is direct communication with the mainstream. Get at those consumers every way possible. Plant the seeds of word-of-mouth buzz by using your customers' experiences and testimonials in your marketing.

Once you create enough word-of-mouth experience-sharing and recommendations among mainstream consumers, you'll tip toward having evangelists. Consumer-to-consumer conversations are a hard place to get to—few companies have attained it, much less a critical mass that's enough to convert consumers into evangelists.

But it's more than possible. Consumers want to love technology. They want to be blown away and tell their friends and family about how great your technology is. Follow the plan in this book to help them to do exactly that.

Chapter Summary

Apple utilizes best-in-class products, industry-leading user experiences, tantalizing events, and a lack of communication with the press to create and carefully manage a constant flow of rumors and information. This is infinitely valuable to them because it is perceived that Apple is not propagating its own buzz but that consumers are!

Apple has created a passionate community ecosystem that includes the major media, bloggers, consumer evangelists, and mainstream consumers who are not yet evangelists. These groups all talk to each and propagate the Apple brand and messaging.

A critical mass of word-of-mouth endorsements, from one mainstream consumer to another, is what tips you from having enthusiastic customers to having evangelistic consumers.

Mainstream word-of-mouth buzz is difficult to attain, but there is magic in it. It has been, and it is, quite attainable. You are holding in your hands the steps you need to execute to get there.

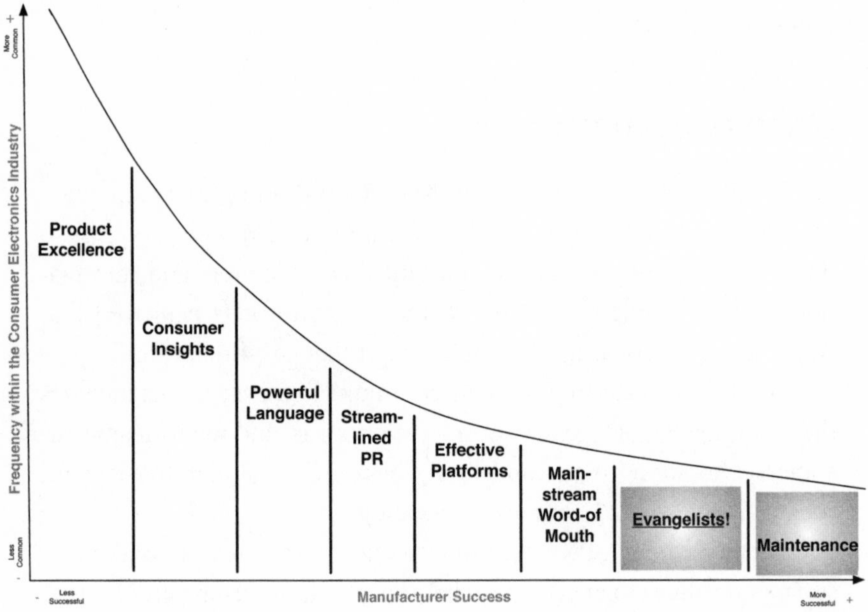

More Common +
Frequency within the Consumer Electronics Industry
Less Common -
Product Excellence
Consumer Insights
Powerful Language
Stream-lined PR
Effective Platforms
Main-stream Word-of Mouth
Evangelists!
Maintenance
- Less Successful
Manufacturer Success
More Successful +

twelve

The Joys of Having Evangelists

In this chapter, let's do a quick review of the steps required to attain evangelists and of all the wonderful things they can do for you. We'll end with a look at what's involved in keeping evangelists because, even though they're your die-hard fans today, they'll change teams tomorrow if you let them get away. The chapter ends with a discussion of how to prevent that. So this is a chapter of three lists that cover how to attain evangelists, what they can do for you, and how to maintain their religious fervor for your company and products.

How to Attain Evangelists

Here is a review of the steps I covered in this book:

- Everything begins with shifting your perspective away from thinking technically toward thinking about the life improvement your products bring. Stop thinking about specs and start thinking about your language and how consumers perceive it.

- Your products must be singular. If they're not, there is no chance of developing passionate consumers—won't happen. Bad products quickly disappear from the market. It's impossible to create energized customers for these products. Your products must be so good that people feel wonderful using them.
- Give your product an interesting, easy-to-remember name.
- Price them within consumers' expectations.
- Attain wide distribution and allow people to purchase your devices quickly and easily.
- Avoid early adopters if possible and dive right into conquering the mainstream consumer market.
- Innovate products and marketing aggressively so people aren't tempted to stray.
- Ruthlessly seek insights about your customers through qualitative conversations.
- Perfect, streamline, and simplify your language. Tell customer results stories.
- Take control of your public relations and media relations. A terrible PR function is literally killing good companies' products.
- Speak directly to consumers by developing effective communications platforms: focus on big media and avoid marketing on social media. Be where the mainstream is.
- Take measures to nurture word-of-mouth recommendations among consumers (even if these word-of-mouth recommendations occur on the dreaded social media networks!). A critical mass of mainstream word-of-mouth buzz launches you into the rarified air of consumer evangelists.

- Finally, and I cover this later, maintain your evangelists by staying aggressive. You cannot rest on your laurels in this business. Gravity pushes backwards. You will not only be passed by if you don't continue to be successful in innovating products and marketing, but you'll simply drop off the consumer radar. It has happened many times in our business, where once-high-flying manufacturers found themselves fighting for survival.

What Evangelists Can Do for You

In the introduction, I detailed the traits of a consumer evangelist. In this section, let's look at what they can do for you.

- They talk about you nonstop. They discuss what they love about the products they own, and also what they hear might be coming soon. They talk about their hopes and dreams for your products with other evangelists. They market for you. They deliver your messaging, often word for word. They excite those around them for you. Want to create buzz about something, real or rumor? Just plant a seed with your evangelist community. It'll germinate and grow.
- They buy your products again and again. They also buy your devices as gifts because they got so much out of them. They buy multiple items from you only because you manufacture them, and they love you.
- They trust you. So if you, say, redesign a popular phone and put antennas on the outside of the phone, which causes a big problem, like, say, reception loss, your evangelists will think it's no big deal to put up with this problem. *So what? Just buy a case.* Remember?
- They will also forgive you quickly for mistakes. Because these consumers are loyal evangelists, they figure your mistake was honest and you're working to fix it,

and who's perfect anyway? Problems blow over much quicker for companies that have evangelists.

- They defend you publicly among their peers and even among strangers. Head to one of the many Apple message boards. There, you will find people complaining about Apple hardware, software, and services. They might blame Apple. They might be angry, which people usually are when something breaks and they head online to complain. Invariably, you'll also see Apple evangelists defending the company, helping the person. If he or she doesn't want to be helped, the evangelists simply keep defending the company. They are a moat around your castle. And when necessary, they're the alligators, too, keeping the enemy at bay.
- Because there are so many of them, they create endless "live demos" of your devices. In airports, on buses or trains, at the coffee shop. And if somebody strikes up a conversation with them, they'll be more than happy to sell your technology to them. Literally.
- They are an incredible sounding board. Companies without evangelists have to read product reviews and seek out customers for feedback. Companies that have attained evangelist consumers hear from them frequently—and there are thousands of blogs and community Web sites where they congregate. They're easy to find, and easier still to learn from.
- They influence the media just as much as, if not more than, the media influences them. Journalists see the huge interest in your products—friends, family, neighbors, colleagues, and strangers. They observe the energy, which is contagious.
- Evangelists improve your retail position. They will get you better placements on shelves—real shelves and online shelves. Evangelists are asking for, and about, your

product. *When are you getting the iPhone? Do you have the iPad?* Retailers hear this and respond.

- They make news for you. They line up around the block when you launch a product. They flock to a new product or service when a new platform (say, Verizon Wireless or the iPad for Netflix) carries it.

How to Maintain Evangelists

Keeping consumer evangelists is as difficult as attaining them. You must keep innovating aggressively—sprinting, not just running—to maintain your highest standing among these people. Your evangelists need to feel like you are working as hard for them as they are for you. Here is how to create those feelings:

- Never stop communicating. Even companies that had evangelists for a long period of time lost them when they stopped talking to people. Palm is one example. Momentum makes mainstream communication relatively easy. But when attempting to begin communicating from a silent (stopped) position, it's nearly impossible to gain traction. You worked incredibly hard to attain these evangelists—the fastest way to lose them is simply to stop talking to them.
- Never stop listening. Hear what they're saying, even if it's not directly to you. But listen to them online and offline and react to what they're saying. If enough of your evangelists have a problem, then you have a problem.
- Keep improving your product without charging people for it. The iPhone keeps getting operating system upgrades. After the major ones, it's like a brand-new phone, for free. Netflix keeps expanding its list of compatible devices, not to mention growing its streaming movie library by what feels like tens of thousands of movies every year. Keep advancing. Keep surprising people with quality.

- Continue to perfect your marketing:
    - → Gather insights from your customers using qualitative interviews.
    - → Perfect your language. Simplify constantly. Make your message more emotional.
    - → Develop powerful, concise ways to explain what your products and services do for people. Create one sentence that communicates your value memorably and immediately for each product.
    - → Streamline your public relations effort. Get your executives involved in managing media relationships. Get the PR team more involved with the strategic direction of your company but less involved with managing the media.
    - → Communicate your message directly to consumers from the right platforms. Avoid using platforms that don't reach the mainstream.

"Keep People Surprised and Pleased with the Service"

❖ ❖ ❖

"Evangelism is nourished by continuing to improve the services, adding titles, adding devices, or making searches easier. Making the product better. Keeping people surprised and pleased with the service. When we slipped and had an outage, we didn't deliver DVDs for two or three days. Most people didn't even notice it. But we gave our customers a 10 percent credit on their bill, without them asking for it. We did it because it was the right thing to do."

—Steve Swasey, vice president of corporate communications, Netflix

Alex's Analysis: Consumers expect excellence from you; that's why they evangelize your company and products. To keep them, you must constantly perfect your excellence.

- Make sure you're communicating your continuous improvements: Apple, Netflix, and Amazon (with the Kindle) do a masterful job at this. Everyone knows when a new product is coming or a new agreement is executed with, for example, the Stars Network for its movies. If your product improvements are done in a vacuum, that's of no help to you.
- Stay ruthlessly focused on the mainstream and on the lifestyle value of your products. If you want to know how to do this, just listen to how Steve Jobs talks about his products. The vast majority of his adjectives are emotional and feeling words: amazing, incredible, powerful, first-ever, awesome, great, etc. They're words that make you feel good.
- Limit your product focus. It's better to be great at one or two things than slightly above average at thirty things. Plus, how do you decide which thing to focus on? History shows that companies with countless products across various industries have a hard time focusing their marketing resources in any one place, so they do not create evangelists. Examples are Sony, Microsoft, and Hewlett-Packard. Conversely, companies that do enjoy consumer evangelists only focus on a handful of products: Amazon just does a couple models of the Kindle, Apple only focuses on a few big consumer products,

and Netflix, obviously, only does two things—DVDs and streaming.

- Give people something to talk about. They're paying attention to you—you've built up a rapt audience. Build their interests and excitement by hinting at what's coming up. Even if you must (deep breath) carefully position a rumor or two about what's to come. Assuming the rumor is accurate of what's to come, there is no downside to this. It only builds buzz.
- Simplify everything: your products, your services, your marketing, your language, your channels, your internal systems. Apple only has a handful of engineers developing their major products at any one time, according to former CEO John Sculley. How many does your company have?

"Constantly Simplify the User Experience"

"It's always about constantly simplifying the user experience. It's about simplifying everything. The advertising must be simplified (look at Apple's). The supply chain must be simplified (Apple has retail stores and a Web site). Sony has 150,000 SKUs [products]. And Apple has a handful. And Apple is worth at least four times as much as Sony. I bet you Sony's CEO never gets involved in product design decisions, and I bet you he doesn't get involved in the marketing of a product. Whereas Steve [Jobs] gets involved in everything. Before you sell the experience, you have to simplify the experience."

—John Sculley, former CEO, Apple

Alex's Analysis: Music to my ears. In this business, where complexity is natural and automatic, simplicity is a proven path to success. Amazon only manufactures and markets one product, the Kindle (I'm not counting those Amazon Basics products). Netflix only focuses on one service. And, obviously, Apple is masterful at pushing just a handful of products forward at once. All three of these companies have also simplified their messaging. They have perfected what they say so that it's immediately understandable. Watch instantly is a phrase now immediately associated with Netflix by many consumers. E-books is a term that brings the Kindle to mind for most. This top-of-mind positioning in the mainstream is a result of simplifying... everything.

We end with the beginning: make amazing products. In a process filled with critical steps, a phenomenal product is the first one.

Chapter Summary

There is a process for attaining evangelists and a separate, related one for maintaining them.

Maintaining evangelists is just as difficult as developing them.

But if you have them, the difficult business of consumer electronics becomes much, much easier.

With consumer evangelists, you have a massive leg up on any competition. In fact, you really elevate yourself above and beyond any competition.

thirteen

The Evangelist Marketing Assessment

I have worked with some of the best-known technology brands in the world and also with small, high-tech startups. And although I am almost always hired by a high-level executive who has the authority to pay me (that person becomes my client), most projects have me interacting with people across all strata of a company. And when I interact with midlevel managers and their teams of associates in marketing and public relations, I often hear the following: *I wish we could influence what we say to people. But we can't. I can't. I have no influence on how we do things. I just do what I'm told.*

Well, this chapter is for you.

It will put the influence squarely into your hands. In fact, it is your influence. I've put together this quick assessment to help you understand where your company falls on the Evangelist Marketing Continuum. Are you talking about your products in the right way? Are you talking to the right people, from the right places? Who is leading your communications? Answer the questions in this assessment, score your results, and take the corresponding findings to your boss. And his boss. And her boss. And show them where your company can improve.

The Assessment

Your Perspective

1. Do you see yourself and your company as being in the life improvement business *instead of* in the engineering business? YES/NO
2. Do you think of yourself and your company as being in the marketing business primarily? YES/NO
3. Do you focus on creating the most passionate customers instead of the most product models? YES/NO
4. Does consumer perception and feedback shape your marketing approach? YES/NO
5. Is your public relations department involved in the early stages of marketing strategy formulation? YES/NO
6. Does your customer base see you as making special or singular products, as opposed to commodities? YES/NO

Your Leadership

1. Does your CEO lead frequent gatherings with the entire company to communicate about your products? YES/NO
2. Does your CEO frequently engage the media and industry observers personally and directly? YES/NO
3. Does your CEO use and repeat powerful, emotional language to describe your product and company? YES/NO
4. Does your CEO have a strong vision of the kind of products he wants the company to create, and can he clearly and quickly articulate how these products will improve people's lives? YES/NO

5. Do your executive leaders set the tone for powerful marketing by using emotional, lifestyle-oriented language about your products? YES/NO
6. Do your high-level executives actively seek out and communicate consumer insights and desires for your products to you? YES/NO

Your Product

1. Is your product functionally good? Does it do what you say it does? YES/NO
2. Do your products make people feel like their quality of life is improved when they use them? YES/NO
3. Do your products make people feel good? YES/NO
4. Are your product names short, simple, and memorable? YES/NO
5. Are your devices priced within consumers' expectations? YES/NO
6. Are your products widely available, online and offline, and easy to buy? YES/NO

Your Product Name

1. Is it short? YES/NO
2. Is it easy to remember? YES/NO
3. Is it easy for consumers to repeat your product name when describing it to their peers? YES/NO
4. Does your product's name follow in the mold of the most successful products' names (iPod, Walkman, TiVo)? YES/NO

Your Customers

1. Do mainstream consumers outnumber highly technical early adopters among your prospect base? YES/NO

2. Do you test your products and messaging on mainstream consumers from launch day, bypassing techie early adopters? YES/NO
3. Would you rate your typical customer as energized about your product and company? YES/NO
4. Do your customers talk to each other about your products? YES/NO

Your Consumer Insights

1. Do you regularly speak to your customers? YES/NO
2. Do you conduct qualitative interviews with your customers to gather deep insights about how they integrate your products into their lives? YES/NO
3. Do your executives speak regularly (even if only briefly) with end users? YES/NO
4. Do your engineers speak regularly with end users? YES/NO
5. Does your company regularly read product reviews online? YES/NO

Your Language

1. Do you use emotional language instead of technical specifications to describe your product? YES/NO
2. Are you using the words of your customers in your communications? YES/NO
3. Do you speak about lifestyle outcomes when discussing your devices? YES/NO
4. Do you tell your customers' stories in your communication? YES/NO
5. Do you communicate with consumers constantly through multiple media? YES/NO

6. Is your messaging simple and easy to understand? YES/NO

Your Public Relations

1. Do you avoid blasting press releases to large numbers of media? YES/NO
2. Are your press release headlines short, tight, interesting, and catchy? YES/NO
3. Do your press releases focus on customers' lifestyle improvements instead of technical specifications? YES/NO
4. Do your press releases tell the stories of happy customers? YES/NO
5. Do you work toward establishing relationships with producers, writers, and editors? YES/NO
6. Do you suggest ideas to media one-on-one? YES/NO
7. Do your executives have relationships with the press? YES/NO

Your Platforms

1. Do you use social media to listen to what your customers are saying? YES/NO
2. Conversely, do you avoid using social media as a marketing and sales tool? YES/NO
3. Do you avoid overemphasizing coverage on technical blogs? YES/NO
4. Instead, do you target big media Web sites and blogs? YES/NO
5. Are you effectively utilizing television, radio, and print to alert consumers about your company and products? YES/NO
6. Is your product packaging as good as the device that's in it? YES/NO

7. Does your product package pop on retail shelves? (Because sometimes that's all you can rely on at retail.) YES/NO
8. Does your product manual actually explain how people can use your device to improve their lives?
9. Is your product manual easy to read? YES/NO

Your Word-of-Mouth Buzz

1. Do you take steps to build and encourage word-of-mouth buzz among your customers? YES/NO
2. Are you building multiple communities of passionate supporters? YES/NO
3. Is the big media one of your communities? YES/NO
4. Do you sometimes hold details back from the media to build interest and mystique? YES/NO

Your Evangelist Maintenance

1. Do you actively nourish and encourage your customer evangelists? YES/NO
2. Do you take steps specifically to surprise and delight your evangelist customers? YES/NO
3. Are you constantly in communication with your evangelist consumers? YES/NO
4. Are you listening to everything your evangelists are saying (even if you ignore some of it)? YES/NO
5. Are you constantly perfecting your products and your marketing to nourish evangelists? YES/NO

Scoring

The scoring for this assessment can be most easily explained this way: the more yesses the better.

First, add up the number of YES answers in each section, and write that number down next to each section. From here, you can see exactly which areas of the Evangelist Marketing system you excel at, and on which ones you need to work.

Then, simply, add up your total number of YESSES. Here's what your number means:

52 or more: More than likely, you have evangelists among mainstream consumers. They may or may not be at a critical mass, but you're doing a lot of things right. Make sure you continue to execute on the actions that you're already implementing. And convert NO steps to YES steps one or two at a time. You've attained some excellent results, but remember, gravity pushes backwards. You must continue doing the small things that got you here and deliberately implement the things you aren't doing.

40-52: You are doing better than most, and are on your way to creating mainstream consumer evangelists. Still, there's work to do—go through the questions in the assessment that you answered NO to and review the corresponding material in this book. Every question is elaborated upon throughout the book. And don't forget to keep doing the good things that have brought you to this point. Remember that if your company does not put energy into the areas that are YESSES now, they'll become NOS soon.

20-39: You have some good building blocks in place, but it's time to reevaluate: Is your product the kind of device that inspires consumer evangelists? Take a look at Chapter 4 again and see if your device has some built-in Feel Good Factor, for example. Do customers perceive that your product improves their quality of life? If so, move on to your product name and pricing. Find the parts of the book that detail the areas you answered NO to and go to work. Remember: move one or two areas forward at a time. Every improvement will have an impact. One step at a time, you'll be moving your brand and your company toward a critical mass of consumer evangelists.

0-19: You should start at the beginning of the system (and book), and evaluate your company mindset. Does staff think of itself as an engineering company or a marketing company? Do you make as many products as possible or as many satisfied customers as possible? Begin to work on shifting your perspective to the right place, then reposition your devices from this new perspective. This is not a terrible place to be because you get to start from the beginning. It's a clean reset. Get to work!

Write to Me

How did you do? Let me know at alex@technologytailor.com. Ask me your questions, too; I'll reply personally.

conclusion

Go Forth, Tell Everyone the Good You Do

Throughout this book, I've been telling you what most consumer electronics companies are doing wrong and offering suggestions and techniques for correcting those issues. But when you boil it down, people love consumer electronics. Your products, at mainstream retail, are generally very good.

Think for a moment about the joy that consumer electronics bring people. We love our smartphones and our HDTVs and our digital cameras. We love our photo-sharing sites and our digital music and our streaming video. We love shopping for it, researching it, learning about it, getting the box, opening it, seeing our new, carefully selected product for the first time, and then putting it to use. In doing so, we bring these products into our homes and families, and we integrate them into our lives.

Your products improve people's lives.

You bring enjoyment to the world.

People love what you make and what you sell.

Now, all that's left to do is to help the quality of your marketing catch up to the quality of the hardware and software that you make.

You just have to put into words the joy that you bring to people.

Define as specifically as possible the good that you bring into the world. Identify it by talking with lots of your customers. Then, tell everyone who will listen.